Quick and Dirty

A Compact Guide to Writing, Reading, and Research

SECOND EDITION

Fred Cooksey

Crooked Pig Press

Easthampton, Massachusetts

CROOKED PIG PRESS
116 Pleasant Street
Suite 49
Easthampton, Massachusetts 01027
413.282.8701

Manufactured in the United States of America.

For Zoe, Betsy, Mom, and Ramona

facebook.com/quickanddirty

CONTENTS

IV ODDS AND ENDS

Preface

Why is it called *Quick and Dirty*?

In case you haven't heard this phrase before, it refers to information that is given efficiently and without excess explanation. That was my goal in writing this book, to give students the information they need about writing, reading, and research quickly, and in simple terms.

On the second edition

This book remains a work-in-progress, and your feedback will help me continue to improve it. What works? What doesn't? What doesn't need to be here? What needs to be expanded or made clearer?

I greatly appreciate any feedback you're able to offer. Contact me at fcooksey@ hcc.edu, or comment at facebook.com/quickanddirty.

Acknowledgements

I would like to thank Mike Walker for his enthusiastic support of this book over the past five years. His thoughtful critiques and generous praise have provided both direction and inspiration.

I would also like to thank my many colleagues in the Holyoke Community College English Department who have used the book in their courses, especially Elizabeth Trobaugh, Kim Hicks, and Deborah Fairman. Their feedback has been essential to the continued improvement of this book.

Finally, thanks to the many students who have offered kind words of encouragement as well as some keen-eyed proofreading.

Fred Cooksey
July 2011

chapter 1

COLLEGE SURVIVAL
OR, WHAT *NOT* TO DO IN YOUR CLASSES

Only the educated are free.
> ~ Epictetus

What does a college degree mean in America today?

A piece of paper.

That's how students often talk about it, and that—in many ways—is how many employers view it.

Particularly in the world of work, a college degree means that you are able to complete a variety of time-consuming, sometimes demanding and sometimes tedious tasks. Some of those tasks will require you to apply every ounce of your intelligence, while others will call only on your ability to memorize trivial information that you will probably forget within a matter of hours.

Finishing college may or may not make you smarter, but it will certainly prove that you have discipline. That's why employers want people with college degrees. When you complete a degree, it communicates to potential employers, "I am able to complete many tasks, even when some of them are not terribly interesting to me personally."

And that's an admirable personal quality, one that you will find useful in any number of real-life situations.

However. This is a big However. What I just described is what college "represents" in our world. That doesn't mean that college can't—and shouldn't—be much more. It *should* make you a deeper and more analytical thinker. It *should* expose you to new ideas that cause you to rethink your understanding of the world. It *should* allow you to approach intellectual and practical problems in more creative and productive ways. It *should* make you a better citizen.

As someone who believes in the ability of college to do all of those things (and more), I'm asking you to try to pursue those high-minded ideals. Avoid courses that ask you only to memorize and regurgitate information. Seek out courses that turn your intellectual world upside-down, that confuse and bewilder and challenge you.

It's worth it.

* * *

So here you are in college. Maybe you're eighteen and just out of high school. Or you took some time off (a year? twenty years?) to work, have a family.

Whoever you are, if you're reading this, it's most likely because you're taking English composition (or "first-year writing," or "freshman comp"—whatever your college calls it).

It's the one course that nearly every college student in America must take. And it's a course that many students dread. But it doesn't have to be that way. Much of that dread, I believe, comes from fear—fear of red "correction" marks (like blood) all over your papers, fear of assignments and directions you don't understand.

That fear is what motivated me to write this book. My goal was to create a brief guide to the most important skills you need to start writing at the college level. For me, that begins with survival skills. Plenty of books suggest "techniques for success," but I find most of the suggestions clichéd : study hard, don't put off assignments till the last minute, take a multivitamin, etc. Instead, I'll tell you what *not* to do. It takes the form of a Top 10 list.

Yes, much of what you'll read over the next couple of pages seems like common sense. But when I began surveying my colleagues about these issues, they had a lot to say, which suggests that more than a few students lack the common sense to avoid these behaviors.

TOP 10 PROFESSOR COMPLAINTS

10. Turning in handwritten work / e-mailing papers

Of course, this applies only if an assignment requires that you turn in a typed or word-processed paper. (Most do.)

Many of us—particularly in English—read a lot of student writing: hundreds, sometimes thousands of pages each semester. Do our eyes a favor and type your work as often as possible. Not only will we appreciate it, but it will make your work look more professional.

About e-mail—some professors will require that you submit papers electronically, and that's fine. But if your professor doesn't give you that option, you should resist the urge to e-mail your paper, even if the professor says she doesn't mind. (She's probably just trying to be nice.)

I became so overwhelmed with papers in e-mail that I stopped giving my e-mail address to students. It might not seem like a big deal to you, but opening your e-mail, opening the attachment (and sometimes reformatting the paper), sending it to the printer, then picking it up in the department office on another hall takes time—time I'd rather give to a student who needs some extra help, or time to look over a lesson plan once more before teaching.

It might seem as if your professors have all the time in the world ("They only teach twelve or fifteen hours a week!!!"), but we don't. Most of us love what we do, but it can be exhausting work, particularly commenting on and grading papers. So think about it before you ask your professor to work harder at it.

9. Telling professor what grade you "need" in the course

This particular complaint falls under a larger category of offenses that are not entirely the fault of students. The bigger problem is that higher education has—at least in some places—taken on qualities of the corporate world, with professors now seen (by some) as needing to "serve" students as if the students were "customers."

Most professors deeply resent that kind of thinking. We like to think of ourselves as "serving" higher and more timeless goals, those that have to do with broadening and deepening of human consciousness and understanding.

When students treat education as a "transaction," one in which students have "equal rights," many professors will object.

When you say, "I really need a B in this course," it sounds as if you're trying to find a way around the work it takes to get that grade. Or that you're questioning our grading standards. Now I'll be the first to admit that we're all over the place when it comes to grading—the paper that would get a B from one professor might get a C- from another. But you can't change that. What you can do is learn what it takes to get the grade you want.

The better way to approach this situation is to change both your thinking and your language. Ask yourself: What's important to this professor? Does she put a lot of emphasis on creativity, or does she seem to be more interested in doing everything "by the book"? Does she talk about grammar issues often in class—if so, then sentence construction is probably important to her. Thinking about these questions might help you understand why you got the grade you did. But if you're still unsatisfied, go to talk to the professor during office hours. Then, you can ask her directly: What could I have done differently in this paper? What would have made it better?

If you present this to the professor as your sincere interest in being a better writer or student (and not just getting a higher grade), most of us are more than willing to help.

8. Talking while professor is talking

Rude, disrespectful.

7. Coming to class without book, paper, pen, etc.

Makes you look like you don't care. And maybe you don't. But that certainly won't reflect well on you when we're grading your papers, tests, etc. I could pretend that we grade everything "in a vacuum," which is to say without thinking about who you are as a person in the classroom. But that would be a lie. It's like anything else in life—you're always making an impression on the people around you. What will yours be?

6. Making excuses and/or failing to take responsibility

You'll find a whole range of humanity among your professors, but I think that many of us tend to be compassionate—at least up to a point. We want to believe you when you tell us your grandmother died and you had to go to her funeral, and we don't want to penalize your paper for lateness as a result.

But this type of scenario puts us in a difficult position. You could be lying to us (we've been lied to in the past, we know that much). If you are, then you're getting away with something, and getting an unfair advantage over your classmates. If you're not lying to us, then probably you deserve a break.

But here's the problem—how do we know the difference? And what about students who are too shy or private to share this kind of information with us?

I often struggle with these questions. And I don't think I'm terribly consistent in how I deal with them. Sometimes I give students a break, sometimes I don't.

The lesson for you is this: If you have a legitimate emergency that affects your performance in a class, talk to your professor. He or she might not make any allowances for you, but many professors do want to know.

The other side of this lesson is this: You don't need to tell your professor about every little thing that goes wrong in your life. We don't need to know that you got a flat tire on the way to school, or that your alarm clock is broken and you can't afford to buy a new one because you just spent all your money on a new tire, or that you were throwing up all night and that's why you didn't write your paper. (Were you throwing up every night for the past three weeks, since the paper was assigned? If so, you should be in a hospital, not standing here talking to me.)

The bottom line is this: Most of your professors are really, really tired of hearing excuses. I know—some excuses are much better than others. That's true. But still, we've heard them all.

5. Packing up papers and books before class is over

Rude, rude, rude. Both to the professor and your classmates. Noisy, distracting. When you do this, you are communicating to all who can see or hear you, "I have declared this class to be finished."

Relax.

4. Missing class / coming to class late / leaving class early

If you only miss class, that might not be a big deal to a lot of professors. But the fact is, it often seems to result in more work for your professor. You have to make up a quiz or test; you want to know what material we covered; you need a handout. Any of those things might seem small, but they take up our time and energy, and I can promise you there are other things we'd rather be doing.

I've been persuaded by one of my colleagues (Victor Katz, professor of art history) that lateness is a worse "crime" than simply missing class. (Most professors, by the way, do not share this view, but I find Victor's argument compelling.)

As Victor says, "Late has victims; absent does not." By this he means that when you're late (or leave early), you interrupt class, which affects both your teacher's ability to teach and your classmates' ability to learn. It doesn't matter how quietly you come in or leave—it's distracting.

3. Asking the professor "Did I miss anything" after an absence

This is obnoxious on so many levels. First, it makes us wonder if you were dropped on your head as a newborn, because the question is just plain dumb. Of course you missed something. You missed *class*, that time during which I attempt to teach you something *every single day*. Second, the question is offensive, because it implies that I might not have actually taught anything—or at least not anything important.

Also, if your syllabus includes a calendar (one that says what material will be covered throughout the semester), this question reveals laziness. Instead of asking me, you could have looked at the syllabus to see what you missed.

The solution: Don't ask this question. Talk to a classmate (before or after class) about what happened, and if you're still not sure what went on, then go talk to the professor during office hours. But don't expect us to go over everything we did. We'll give you a brief summary of the subject(s) we covered, and then it's your responsibility to figure out how to learn that material.

This is true even if you had an excellent reason for missing class. We simply can't recreate a 50- or 75-minute class for every student who's absent.

2. Not reading

More and more often, it seems, students are coming to class without having done assigned reading. Maybe you figure the professor will be "going over" that article or chapter, so there's no point in reading it in advance.

Here's the irony of this development: For the last twenty or so years, professors have been encouraged to lecture less and involve students in classroom discussions more. Many of us have moved in this direction, but now, when we try to have an actual discussion about a reading assignment, it often falls flat because half the class (or more) hasn't done the reading.

In terms of being educated, there's nothing more important than reading. Not browing, not checking the Spark Notes, not googling a summary—just good old-fashioned reading.

1. Using cell phones / texting

Most of your professors went to college before the cell phone era. This may be part of why we hate them so much, at least during class.

Here's the thing—it's not easy to teach well. (Think about how hard it is when you have to stand in front of class for a five-minute presentation.) Most of us try to make our material interesting and to provoke critical thinking. The sound of a ringing cell phone is such a jarring disruption that we tend to lose our train of thought, and then more than just a few seconds are lost.

And then there's texting. We don't like that either. It might not make any noise, but it's still distracting, both to us and your classmates. And yes, we see you with your hands inside your jacket pockets or under your desk, and we know from the glazed look on your face that you're not paying attention.

Please, please, please—my colleagues and I are begging you—turn off all the electronic devices before class starts.

* * *

FINAL THOUGHTS

These complaints might have struck you as negative, or at least a bit cranky. I hope not. Like I said, most professors love what we do and wouldn't trade jobs with anyone. But even the most even-tempered and tolerant among us can get irritated with students who seem clueless about how to behave in a college class. The lesson is the same for college as it is for much of life—think about how your actions and attitudes are affecting people around you. Don't do it because it will make *my* life easier; do it because it will make *your* life in my classroom easier.

* * *

In the interest of fairness, I would like to hear from you. Email your complaints about professors (no names, please) to

fcooksey@hcc.edu

I'll consider compiling these for the next edition of this book or for inclusion in an instructor's manual to accompany the text.

The last thought I'll leave you with here is a more positive one: Your professors want you to succeed. We want you to be smarter and more confident. We want good things for you.

That's why I included the list.

facebook.com/quickanddirty

(but not during class)

chapter 2

READING AND CRITICAL THINKING

Too often students are given answers to remember,
rather than problems to solve.

> ~ Roger Lewin

All writing is rhetorical. This is a popular saying among English teachers. What it means is that writers are always trying to get the reader to see things their way. I'm challenging you, in this chapter, to think about how writers make rhetorical decisions that—they hope—will cause you to agree with the "world" they're presenting in their writing.

In college, you'll be asked to read three basic types of writing: informative, argumentative, and literary. The difference between informative and argumentative writing may seem obvious, but often it isn't—mainly because many writers who are trying to get you to see things their way are good at presenting their views as, seemingly, information or fact. So, even when you're reading an article or essay that appears to be plainly informative, you should be aware of how the writer may be "positioned" on a particular issue. In other words, she may have a stance or point of view that she wants you to accept.

TIP Ethos, pathos, and logos: These are the three ways in which Aristotle claimed that speakers persuade their audience. They apply equally well to writing, and you should be aware of how they operate on you as a reader. *Ethos* is an "ethical" appeal to the reader; it means that the writer is presenting herself as trustworthy and believable: "I have a degree from Yale, and my research has been published in many scholarly journals, so you should trust me." *Pathos* is an emotional appeal, one that is meant to evoke feelings of sympathy from the reader: "The chimpanzee had a look of fear and panic in his eyes before the test began." *Logos* is a rational, logical appeal, one that depends on reason: "If scientists are prevented from conducting tests on animals, research into traumatic brain injuries will end."

INFORMATIVE VS. ARGUMENTATIVE WRITING

Informative Writing

- Most textbooks
- Newspaper and magazine "reportage": the articles that present the news but don't comment on it*

Argumentative Writing

- Editorial and opinion pages in newspapers
- "Elite" magazine articles and commentary
- Most nonfiction books (even those that rely largely on facts tend to be "positioned"; there are very few books that do nothing but present "facts"—almost all will also *interpret* the facts)

In college, you'll be reading for a few different reasons: to gather information that you might be tested on, as background for a topic that you discuss in class, or as research for a paper. In any case, you'll almost always need to be able to take away two basic things from your reading: purpose and support.

TIP Pay attention to the first and last paragraphs. Most essays will reveal their purpose in the first paragraph or two, and often return to it in the final paragraph. Note: Some essays will begin by telling a story or doing something slightly unconventional, but in these cases the paragraphs that follow will state the purpose more clearly.

INFORMATIVE WRITING: ARTICLE IN DAILY NEWSPAPER

On the next page, you'll find the beginning of two articles that appeared the morning after Barack Obama was elected president. The first is from the *Wall Street Journal*, a paper known for its conservative values and emphasis on economic issues. The second article is from the *New York Times*, a paper generally regarded as more liberal. My analysis to the right explains some basic features of the articles and makes some comparisons betweeen them.

---

* Journalism is often criticized for being biased. Critics say that the bias begins when editors choose which events to cover, and that it continues when reporters decide which details to use or omit. Think about these questions as you compare the coverage of Obama's election in the *New York Times* and the *Wall Street Journal*.

Article—*Wall Street Journal*

Obama Sweeps to Historic Victory

Sen. Barack Obama was elected the nation's first African-American president, defeating Sen. John McCain decisively Tuesday as citizens surged to the polls in a presidential race that climaxed amid the worst financial crisis since the Great Depression.

My Analysis

This is essentially factual and straight-forward; some may say that focusing the end of the sentence on the financial crisis implies that this is the reason why Obama won. Many other newspapers attributed Obama's success, at least in part, to voters' dissatisfaction with George Bush. This is an example of how the selection of facts can influence how we perceive "reality."

Article—*New York Times*

Obama Elected President as Racial Barrier Falls

Barack Hussein Obama was elected the 44th president of the United States on Tuesday, sweeping away the last racial barrier in American politics with ease as the country chose him as its first black chief executive.

The election of Mr. Obama amounted to a national catharsis—a repudiation of a historically unpopular Republican president and his economic and foreign policies, and an embrace of Mr. Obama's call for a change in the direction and the tone of the country.

My Analysis

Notice how the Times writers choose to focus on the issue of race rather than economics.

Even more of a contrast to the Wall Street Journal *article can be found in the second paragraph, where the* Times *writers assert that voters experienced a catharsis (a release of strong emotions) in choosing Obama. A catharsis suggests that voters were finally able to release all of their pent-up dissatisfaction with Bush; of course, only some voters had such strong feelings about Bush.*

ARGUMENTATIVE WRITING: EDITORIAL IN DAILY NEWSPAPER

Below, on the left, is the beginning of the *Wall Street Journal's* editorial (an opinion essay written by the newspaper's editors) on the election of Barack Obama; it appeared November 5, 2008. Because it's an editorial, no authors are listed—it was written by the *Journal's* editorial board.

Editorial—*Wall Street Journal*

My Analysis

Headline: President-elect Obama

Hearty congratulations to President-elect Barack Obama. The American electorate has handed him and his fellow Democrats the kind of sweeping victory they haven't had since at least 1976 and in certain respects since 1964. We'll now find out if the Democratic Party has learned anything since the last two times it held all the levers of power in Washington.

Any Presidential victory is partly personal, and certainly this one is a credit to Mr. Obama's rhetorical skills and unique appeal.

Note the use of the word "handed"—it suggests that neither he nor other Democrats earned their victories, and that Americans did not fully think through what they were doing.

*Notice what they're **not** saying— that Obama had good ideas, or that he deserved his victory. Mentioning his "unique" appeal downplays what others have called his charisma.*

Critical thinking

Find the entire editorial online and read it. Identify differences in language and tone between the editorial and the news story ("Obama Sweeps to Historic Victory"). Pay particular attention to the use of verbs.

Further study: Find other newspapers' (such as the *Los Angeles Times*, the *Washington Post*, or your local paper) coverage of the election. Search the date of publication (November 4 or 5, 2008) at the paper's archives. Compare organization, selection of details, and use of language.

TYPES OF WRITERS

WHO ARE YOU READING?

You'll have an advantage in understanding what you read if you know more about some different types of writers—and what their differences mean for you as a reader.

For example, let's say you read this sentence in an online news site:

Eating cereal for breakfast is far healthier than eating nothing.

Fine, you think—that sounds reasonable. Your first instinct is to believe the statement. But who wrote it?

The author's name (I'm making this all up to illustrate a point) is Jason Yost. You've never heard of him.

Now, how would you feel about that piece of "information" if Jason Yost were

    a. a researcher in nutrition science at Yale University
    b. a stay-at-home dad who dropped out of college because his girlfriend got pregnant when they were 22
    c. the president of a company that owns five major cereal manufacturers

The answer makes a huge difference in how we interpret the information. This is primarily because of two factors: motivation and qualification.

Motivation

Both the Yale researcher and the stay-at-home dad might be motivated by the search for truth; both might desire to advance our understanding of nutrition.

But the company president is most likely motivated by the desire to sell more cereal. Whatever "the truth" might be, the company president is far more likely to manipulate it so that it serves his needs.

Qualification

Like many things in life, this is not an "either-or" question. Think of it instead as being on a continuum, like this:

Not at all qualified   **Somewhat qualified**   **Highly qualified**

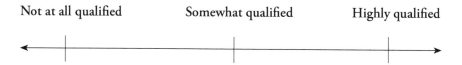

In our example, the Yale researcher is highly qualified, the stay-at-home dad is probably not at all qualified, and the company president—who knows? You'd have to find out about his credentials.

Sometimes it's not so simple to determine what kind of writer you're reading, so first I'll describe some of the basic types of writers you're likely to encounter. In case it's not confusing enough, keep in mind that not all writers fit neatly into these categories. For example, a writer might be a scholar when she publishes papers and books about marine biology—but when she publishes an opinion piece in the *New York Times*, she's both a scholar and an opinion writer.

REPORTERS / JOURNALISTS

Reporters typically work for newspapers and magazines. Generally, they are not specialists in any particular field—rather, they know how to gather information (usually via interviews) and put it together in a way that can be understood by a broad audience. It's also true, though, that at the best newspapers, most reporters are extremely knowledgeable about more specific areas, e.g. Congress, the automotive industry, education, etc.

OPINION WRITERS

This category includes people who write editorials, columns, and other opinion pieces. Their work can be found in newspapers, magazines and online publications (like Slate.com, Salon.com, and many others). Often—particularly in newspapers—these writers were once reporters.

When you read opinion writers, it's important to distinguish between those who are "generalists" and those who are "experts." Most opinion writers are generalists—meaning that they typically write about a range of issues, none of which they are "expert" in. For example, a newspaper columnist might write an essay about global warming—and it might be quite well-researched and persuasive—even though he or she never did college or graduate coursework in environmental science, geology, meteorology, etc.

Sometimes, opinion writers *are* experts. Look for a biographical note about the author that explains who the person is; often this will state where the person works, which should reveal a lot. For example, a recent biographical note in the *New York Times* says: "John Farmer, a former attorney general of New Jersey and senior counsel to the 9/11 commission, teaches at Rutgers Law School." The writer, clearly, is an expert on law, which is the subject of his commentary. It doesn't mean he's right, of course—but it does mean that he should know matters of law that a generalist typically wouldn't.

SCHOLARS

Scholars have been educated (usually through the PhD level) in a specific field, such as sociology, philosophy, English, physics, and so on. Furthermore, most Ph.D.-level work is highly specialized, with the result that the scholar is focused largely on a particular part of his or her field. Within English, for example, that might mean eighteenth-century Russian poetry, or post-war American fiction.

When you read a scholar writing in his or her field, you should expect to encounter a high level of language and perhaps some jargon specific to the field. There will likely be numerous references to other research done in the field, as well as footnotes and/or endnotes and a bibliography.

PROFESSIONAL WRITERS

That word *professional* might not be the best choice—but I want it to convey that the writer is an employee, typically of a large company or institution. Unlike a reporter, the professional writer's goal is not (necessarily) to tell the truth; instead, it's to depict the company or organization in the most flattering light. This doesn't necessarily mean that the writer is going to lie to you. But it's frequently the case that these writers stretch, twist and manipulate facts so that the reader will be sympathetic to the company or organization.

Sometimes you'll find these writers in reputable publications such as the *New York Times* and other newspapers and magazines, many of which will include a biographical note such as, "John Smith is Chief Information Officer for Blandwood College." Or... "John Smith is the director of security for Giant Computer Systems."

When you see something like that, you should read the author with the understanding that John Smith's first allegiance is not to you, the reader, or to "the truth," but to the organization that pays his salary. When in doubt, do a quick Google search for the author to find out where he works.

CREATIVE WRITERS

These include poets, novelists, short story writers, and some essayists. Many have extensive formal education, while some have little. But we don't look to creative writers for "information"; rather, we read them in order to deepen our understanding of "the human condition."

TYPES OF PUBLICATIONS

Now that you know something about the basic types of writers you're likely to encounter, you should know something about the various publications you might find them in:

- The Internet (I'm leaving this broad purposefully)
- Online news sites
- "Popular" (or general-interest) magazines
- Daily newspapers (including online versions)
- "Elite" magazines
- Scholarly journals

THE INTERNET

You know, of course, what the Internet is, but you should be aware of the great range of materials to be found there. In short, start to think about how you determine which sites are trustworthy and reliable—because many of them aren't. See Chapter 8: Internet Research for more information.

ONLINE NEWS SITES

Again, there's a wide range here, and you should pay attention to who's responsible for the material you're reading. For example, if you find a news story on msn.com, it most likely comes from AP (the Associated Press, generally a trustworthy source of information). But often when you click on a link, you're taken to a "story" that is produced by a smaller, less reliable organization. Occasionally you'll be taken to an advertisement rather than an actual news story.

Basic advice: If the link takes you to a story by AP, Reuters, or a major daily newspaper, it's probably reliable.

"POPULAR" AND/OR GENERAL INTEREST MAGAZINES

What I call popular, or general-interest, magazines are those that have large circulations and are read by a wide range of people. Like newspapers, most of the writing in these magazines is done by reporters. But you will also find plenty of opinion writing—so you'll need to be able to tell the two apart.

If you're considering using popular magazines such as *Time*, *Newsweek* and *U.S. News and World Report* as sources for a paper, be aware that they are not highly respected in the academic world. As background information to help you understand the basics of a topic that is unfamiliar to you, these magazines are fine. But if you're looking for depth of analysis, you won't find it here.

DAILY NEWSPAPERS (INCLUDING ONLINE VERSIONS)

Newspapers have played an important role in our country's history, and in democracy in general. (The United States has the strongest protections for freedom of speech—and the press—in the world.)

In the last few years, other forms of "journalism," like blogging, have become powerful too, but there are good reasons to look to newspapers—both for information and for argument.

When you read a newspaper (whether on paper or online), you must know if what you're reading is news or opinion. To do so, it helps to know the differences among the three major "parts" of a daily newspaper: news, editorial and advertising.

News Includes articles about recent events, trends, or people (these should not contain opinions, but many media critics say that even "factual" articles tend to show the reporter's bias)

Editorial Includes editorials, opinion essays, and columns, usually about timely issues

Advertising Sells ads to individuals and companies (this is how newspapers make money—which they've had a hard time doing over the last 10 or 15 years).

Typically, those three departments remain totally separate from each other—because you wouldn't want, for example, the advertising department to be able to say to the news department, "Don't run that story on contaminated beef; we have $100,000 worth of beef advertising this month."

Something to think about....

The highest goals of journalism have always been accuracy and objectivity. (Objectivity means that you're not influenced by your own biases.) Then some philosopher decided that "objectivity" was impossible, that no matter how objective we may strive to be, we will always be influenced by our biases, our particular intellectual and emotional history. The philosopher was probably right, but this idea has caused people—in my opinion, at least—to become unreasonably suspicious of journalists. Yes, some journalists twist the news to fit their political agenda, but I'd like to believe that most reporters simply try to report the news as factually and clearly as possible. In other words, with objectivity as their goal. Just because it's philosophically impossible doesn't mean that reporters don't still strive for it.

Now, having said all that, I'd also say that when you read *anything*, you should watch for subtle cues that the writer has a bias.

TIP **Read analytically.** When you're reading a book or magazine and you're about to turn the page, guess what the word or phrase on the next page will be. After you turn the page, compare what you predicted to what the writer actually wrote. What's different, and why? On the next page, for example, what do you think the next words will be after "'Peer-reviewed' means that experts in the field . . ."?

"ELITE" MAGAZINES

"Elite" is a category I made up because I think these sources differ in important ways from the popular magazines.

First, though, the similarities; like popular magazines, the elites

- can be found (generally) in mainstream bookstores
- are for-profit, with their main source of revenue from advertising
- are published weekly, bi-weekly, or monthly

Now, the differences are important, and they have to do mainly with the way the elites cover the news and issues of the day.

The elites

- print longer articles that go into far more depth
- cover issues that are more complex and less focused on entertainment
- use language that is more sophisticated

Here are some of the magazines that I would include in this group:

> *The New Yorker*
> *Atlantic Monthly*
> *Harper's Monthly*
> *The New York Times Magazine* *
> *The American Scholar*
> *The Nation*
> *The Economist*

While these publications do not have the same standing as scholarly journals, they are widely respected.

* Yes, the *New York Times Magazine* is part of a newspaper, but the articles and essays published in it tend to be more like those in the other elite magazines. It is only published on Sundays.

SCHOLARLY JOURNALS

No matter what field you're in, you're going to have to read scholarly journals, so you should understand something about why they're so important to the academic world.

First, though, here's how they're different from magazines (both popular and elite):

- Almost all are published by a college or university.
- Most do not accept advertising.
- Articles tend to be less timely than those found in magazines and newspapers.
- Few include images or photographs.
- All of the writing is done by scholars in the field.
- The audience is other scholars in the field.
- Many of the articles use language and/or jargon specific to the field.

What this means is that journal articles will typically be challenging to read, particularly early in your college experience.

Only one other piece of information is important to know about journals before you start using them, and that is that they fall into two categories, those that are peer-reviewed and those that are not. Peer-reviewed journals are the most trusted and reliable sources available. "Peer-reviewed" means that experts in the field (for example, leading scholars of abnormal psychology for the journal *Abnormal Psychology*) read and review all articles before they are published. These reviewers tend to be extremely picky about how arguments are constructed, how evidence is presented, and so on. As a result, peer-reviewed journal articles should be absolutely trustworthy.

This is not to say that their content will be absolutely *true*. It only means that they shouldn't contain any blatant errors or misrepresentations of fact.

WARNING: MIND GAMES AHEAD

Passive Voice

Mistakes were made.

> ~ Presidents Reagan, Bush (senior), Clinton, Bush (younger)

Passive is the opposite of active. Grammatically, this means that the writer switches the subject and the object in a sentence, which forces the verb to change:

> Active: The boy hit the ball.
> Passive: The ball was hit by the boy.

In active voice, the "true" subject (the boy) of the sentence is first, and it performs the action. This is the most common way of forming sentences in the English language. When you switch it to passive voice, the meaning is exactly the same, at least in this example. But it's a less natural way for us to read the information. That's the main reason to avoid passive voice as a writer. (Note: I'm not saying you should never use passive voice—only that you should know that you're doing it, and do it for a good reason.)

Sometimes, writers use passive voice because it allows them to omit the "true" subject, the person or thing doing the action, as is the case in the quote above: "Mistakes were made." This statement has become famous—and something of a joke among people who follow politics and/or language—because it has been used by all of our recent presidents to avoid taking responsibility. It should make us ask, *By whom* were mistakes made? But often we don't.

In short, passive voice is not just a grammatical issue—it's also an *ethical* one; here's an example that's closer to your world:

Passive: Tuition and fees at the college were raised.

Active: The college's Board of Trustees raised tuition and fees.

In the passive voice, the sentence omits an important piece of information: *who* is responsible for the increase in tuition and fees. As a result, we don't know whom to blame—or maybe it never even occurs to us to wonder who's responsible for this. We simply accept it.

Pay attention to how politicians and businesses use language (particularly when they are doing something *to* us), and you'll see that they love the passive voice because it allows them to imply that things simply happen, and that no one has caused them to happen.

EVASIVE LANGUAGE: THE ETHICS OF COMMUNICATION

In each of the following examples, you can certainly figure out what's being said. But it takes some effort. The companies that write this "legalese" are counting on you being lazy—they don't want to make it easy for you to understand how to return the digital camera you bought from them or how to cancel your cable service.

In each example below, think about how much more direct the phrasing in the "translation" is, thus leaving no possibility of misinterpretation.

An electronics store (now bankrupt—serves them right)

Original: Due to most manufacturer's policies, final sale items listed above may only be returned directly to the manufacturer.

Translation: You must return final sale items directly to the manufacturer, not to our store.

A rental car company

Original   Purchase of personal accident insurance (PAI) and personal effects coverage (PEC) is optional and not required to rent a vehicle.

Translation   You are not required to purchase personal accident insurance (PAI) or personal effects coverage (PEC) in order to rent a vehicle.

A cable TV company

Original

Refunds/Credits will be given only when request for cancellation of service is received by Charter within 45 days of installation of service (30 days subscribing to the service, plus 15 day grace period for formal requests of refund/credit). Only 30 days of service will be refunded or credited.

Translation

We will only give you a refund or credit if you cancel your Charter service within 45 days of installation (30 days after you subscribed, plus a 15 day grace period). We will only refund or credit 30 days of service.

The last two examples are clumsy and misleading in their original form mainly due to the use of nominalizations—words that could have been verbs but are turned into nouns. Above, the first words (purchase and refunds/credits) are nominalizations. Academic writers and lawyers seem to love nominalizations too, but this appears to be changing—many editors and legal experts are now demanding clearer, more direct language. See end of Chapters 5 for a more thorough explanation.

The lesson

Be alert to the complex ways in which writers try to manipulate you. It will help you become a better student—and a better citizen.

chapter 3

WRITING AS PROCESS

The work will teach you how to do it.

~ Estonian Proverb

All writers have a process—a way of taking loose, unorganized ideas and turning them into words on a page that a reader can interact with. Experienced writers know that "writing" is never as simple as typing up some ideas, turning them into sentences and paragraphs, and running spell-check.

This chapter offers some advice about process, but it's worth remembering that good writers rarely follow these steps exactly as I outline them. Instead, they tend to write in a way that has been described as *recursive*—meaning, roughly, that they go both forward and backward. So they might go from brainstorming to drafting, and then back to brainstorming. Then, they might choose to revise a small portion of their writing so that it says exactly what they want it to, then go back to drafting again.

THE MYTH OF EASY WRITING Every day we read the work of professional writers in newspapers, magazines, and books. Because we only see the finished product—the thing that has been revised and edited (often numerous times)—we might think that the writer simply sat down and typed it. I can assure you that this is almost never the case. Even the most gifted writers have to revise. In most cases, the finished product that we read has little in common with the writer's first draft.

Certainly, writing comes more naturally to some people than others. But even for those people, writing is rarely easy. And it almost never comes without effort. Read what three writers have to say about their process in Chapter 12.

Here's the basic process, in the order I'll discuss it in this chapter:

1. Find your topic
2. Narrow your topic
3. Brainstorm / prewrite
4. Create a thesis (or not)
5. Work from an outline (or not)
6. Draft
7. Revise
8. Proofread

Note: I'm assuming that you've already done some reading and research to prepare for the writing.

FIND YOUR TOPIC

All of your college writing begins with some kind of assignment. Do yourself a favor and pay close attention to it. Make sure you know what's expected of you, and reread the assignment occasionally when you're in the process of writing the paper to make sure you're doing what it calls for.

If your topic has been assigned to you, skip to Brainstorming.

If the choice of topic is up to you, start by thinking about some aspect of the big issues that the class has been addressing. Let's say, for example, that you're taking art history, and you've been told simply to "write a 5-page paper that addresses some issue of modern art."

Three Suggestions

Think about which class sessions you found most interesting. Go back and look at your notes for names of artists, titles of works, other influences on the period.

Freewrite about the broad subject—write down anything that comes to mind about modern art, with the goal only of following your interests.

Explore the subject in books, articles, or the Internet (see Ch. 8 for guidelines). Don't think of this as research yet; instead, think of it simply as a way of exploring the subject in order to find a workable topic. (But do keep track of sources you find in case you want to come back to them later when you do have a topic.)

NARROW YOUR TOPIC

Start with a basic principle: If people have written entire books about your topic, it's not narrow enough. Instead of writing about technology and education, for example, narrow it down to how technology is changing higher education—or, more narrowly still, how Powerpoint is overused in college classrooms.

One of my students recently began with the idea to write about veteran's issues and higher education. To help him narrow that topic, I asked him to talk about some of those issues. He mentioned a number of concerns, but the one that he seemed most interested in was the G.I. Bill (a government program that pays college expenses for those who served in the military a certain number of years). Even that was a bit too broad, so he eventually focused on the current overhaul of the bill, often called G.I. Bill 2.0, taking the position that the revisions to the previous bill were unfair to veterans.

Some of the ideas for brainstorming on the next couple of pages can also help you narrow your topic.

BRAINSTORM / PREWRITE

Opinions seem to come easily to us, but well-constructed essays that explore a subject thoroughly and intelligently—these are less easy, and that's where brainstorming can help.

The key to brainstorming is to learn how to outsmart your brain. (See "Your Brain as Obstacle" on page 27 for more on why this is necessary.) Two techniques—freewriting and clustering—are often helpful when you're trying to generate ideas or find direction for your writing.

CLUSTERING

This technique is good for people who are visual. It can be done on a piece of paper (the larger the better), but it is often most successful when done on a big board with many people contributing.

As with other forms of brainstorming, the key is not to limit the flow of ideas. Still, there's a little more critical thinking involved in clustering, because it does depend on making logical connections among ideas.

CLUSTERING / MAPPING

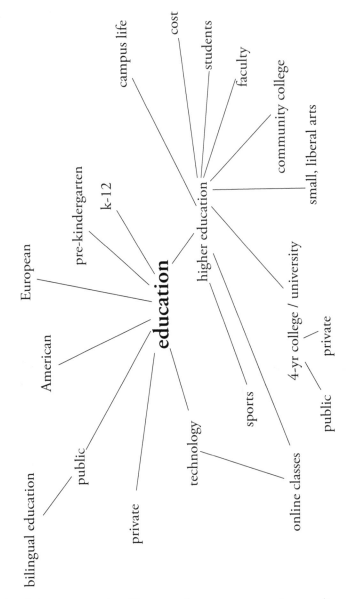

A couple of things to notice: If your web starts to move in one direction (as mine does toward higher education issues), you might start over with "higher education" in the middle and begin branching out again. Also, think about how pieces of this web could be connected. Connecting technology, cost, and online classes, for example, could lead to a good topic about how these issues are changing college life.

Here's how it works. Start with any idea or topic—try to express it in a single word, or two words at most. For this example, I'll use *education*. (See facing page.) Next, think of ways to divide that subject into many parts, aspects, or issues—maybe ask yourself some of the reporter's questions on the next page.

FREEWRITING

One of the simplest ways to generate ideas for a paper is freewriting. The basic idea of freewriting is this: Write (or type—whichever you can do faster and most easily) quickly and without worrying about whether your ideas are good or whether they make sense. Don't worry about grammar. This isn't writing that you'll turn in—it's just a way to help you figure out what you're specifically interested in and some questions you might have about your topic.

Your brain has many parts, and understanding how they contribute to—and get in the way of—writing might help you. I'm no expert on the brain, but I do understand three of its most important functions: it stores memories and other information, it processes emotions, and it reasons.

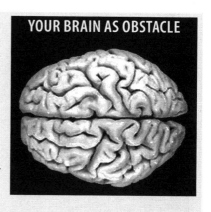

YOUR BRAIN AS OBSTACLE

All of these functions are useful, of course, but not all are equally useful at every stage of the writing process. For example, the part of your brain that is capable of reasoning is essential as you move through the middle and later stages of writing—but you don't necessarily want too much of this kind of brain activity in the early stages of writing. Why? Because that's where the Critic lives. He (or she) is inside your brain, where he remembers your past experiences of writing and stops your thought process to tell you that your writing is no good, your ideas are worthless, etc. (When the Critic is active, she is using all parts of your brain—especially the memories and emotions of past negative experiences with writing.)

Enough psychotherapy. The point is simply to keep in mind that we all have self-critical instincts, even the most (seemingly) well-adjusted people. Those instincts are not productive for you in the early stages of writing, so you should do everything you can to keep them in check.

What to do when you're freewriting

- Ask questions about your topic
- Try to connect different parts of the topic that interest you
- Consider using some of the reporter's questions below

What *not* to do when you're freewriting

- Worry about grammar or spelling
- Edit yourself
- Delete anything

Final thoughts on brainstorming

You'd be surprised how often something useful can come out of what seems like a bad idea. Some of the best ideas come after initially thinking, *That can't possibly*

REPORTER'S QUESTIONS The reporter's five "W" questions are who, what, when, where, why (there's also an "H": how), and they can help you break a big topic down into smaller parts. These questions can also help you make connections among the parts. Not all of the W's are equally effective—in this case, applying the questions to education, I don't think the *why* question is helpful, but I included one question anyway.

Here's an example of applying the reporter's questions to the topic of education.

Who　　Students, professors, administrators, parents, school boards, legislators

What　　Private vs. public, pre-Kindergarten, grade school, high school, higher education.

When　　Different time periods, such as 18th century, early 20th century, 1970s, etc.

Where　　Rural versus urban or suburban schools, even American versus European or other geographic regions.

Why　　Origins of education: Why did education become "formalized"?

How　　Methods of educating people, for example whole langage versus phonics for debates about how students learn to read, or lecture versus "student-centered" instruction in college courses.

work. Don't limit yourself to what you think can be done or what you think will be good.

Think about how creative many kids are—they invent games and "pretend" worlds all the time. Why? Because their imaginations are not limited by some "higher" voice telling them that their games are useless or poorly constructed. They just adapt the games, refine them, discard them, and so on. But they keep inventing.

Invention comes largely from a sense of play and often from lucky accidents. If you follow the rules all the time, the imaginative and inventive parts of your brain will never get a chance to function.

CREATE A THESIS

Once you have some direction for your paper, you should start working on a thesis. (This isn't always true—in some cases, it makes more sense to begin with questions and uncertainties and allow yourself to discover the thesis later.)

Topic vs. Thesis

Your topic is what the paper is about; your thesis is what you have to say *about* the topic. It's your position, your attitude, your stance, your view.

Think of it this way—readers can't disagree with you about your topic. But some readers should be able to disagree with you about your thesis. In this chapter I'll also describe the thesis as your paper's "big purpose."

Sample topic

Portable electronic devices (cell phones, laptops, etc.) in college classes

How would a reader disagree with that? I can't say, "That topic doesn't exist." (I could, but I'd be wrong; when you think of "the reader," you have to imagine a sane, rational person.) I could say, "But portable electronice devices haven't had any effect on college classes"—but again, I'd be wrong, or at least somewhat irrational.

Sample thesis

The presence of portable electronic devices in college classrooms has changed the way students and professors interact.

Not many people would argue with this, of course, but an argument against this assertion is possible. Therefore, it's an acceptable thesis statement. If your professor wants a more argumentative paper, your thesis could look like this:

> The presence of portable electronic devices in college classrooms has adversely affected the way students and professors interact.

A good thesis statement should

- take a postion
- open up a discussion or continue a "conversation"
- be specific

For example, let's say that you're in an anthropology class that's examining the many languages around the world that are in decline—experts say that of the roughly 6700 languages used throughout the world, half are in in danger of "extinction," and one "dies" approximately every two weeks. You would not want a thesis that attempts to take on this very sizable topic. Instead, perhaps, examine a specific language that is considered "endangered." Let's take Irish (or Gaelic, as it's also known) as an example. A more specific thesis statement might investigate whether funding for Irish language television programming is (or is not) merely slowing the inevitable death of the language. That would be sufficiently narrow and specific, and it would also continue a discussion that linguists, Irish people, government officials, and educators have had about the state of the language, and what might or should be done to preserve it.

WORK FROM AN OUTLINE (OR NOT)

Different writers have different approaches to drafting. Some like to have a complete outline that breaks down every single element of the paper, and others would feel far too constrained by such a plan. At some point in the writing process, it's generally smart to write at least a basic, informal outline.

AN INFORMAL OUTLINE

An outline doesn't have to be formal. It can be as simple as this:

1. Introduction, with thesis statement
2. Major point #1
3. Major point #2
4. Major point #3
5. Conclusion

That's the dreaded five-paragraph structure, which many teachers of writing despise. They say that it's too simplistic and limiting. I would argue, though, that many great pieces of writing use some version of this structure, and that most argumentative writing moves through at least two major points that prove the thesis. Also, the simplicity of the structure does not necessarily have to limit the complexity of your argument or the intelligence of your thinking.

In short, you might want to think of this not as a five-paragraph form, but as a *five-part* form where the parts can vary in length. In a simple, three-page paper, the parts would likely be paragraphs. But in a 15-page research paper, each "part" would be a number of pages, made up of many paragraphs.

A FORMAL OUTLINE

If you're one of those hyper-organized people who has to have every last detail of things planned, this is for you. (Or maybe you should avoid it—because it might do you good to approach writing in a different way.)

A formal outline uses Roman numerals and letters. One of the most basic rules is that if you have a 1 (or an A), you must have a 2 (or a B).

I. **Introduction**—background: how education has changed in response to technology
   Thesis: Although many people are critical of online learning, it can be beneficial for all involved. (This is an acceptable "starter" thesis but would need to be refined in the actual paper.)

II. Advantages for the college
   A. Uses no classroom space
   B. Reduces maintanence costs
   C. Requires no additional parking lots

III. Advantages for faculty
   A. More efficient
   B. Convenient

Note: I've only expanded part of the the fourth section.

IV. Advantages for students
   A. Convenient
      1. Better for busy students
         a. Some are parents
         b. Many work
      2. Easy for those with disabilities
   B. Less intimidating

The subpoints (#1 and #2) give evidence for the larger point ("convenient").

These points explain and/or illustrate the subpoint ("Better for busy students").

V. Conclusion

TIP: WORD PROCESSING

Saving as RTF (Rich Text Format)

Computers can be unpredictable, especially when you're moving from home to school or a friend's house to work on a paper, print, etc. I highly recommend that you save your drafts in Rich Text Format, which will ensure that you can open your paper on any computer. If you're using an earlier version of Word, see appendix, page 236.

1. When you're ready to save, click on the Windows logo at the top left corner of screen.

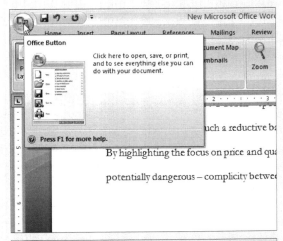

2. Choose **Save As** from the pull-down menu (rather than just **Save**, which would leave the document in Word format).

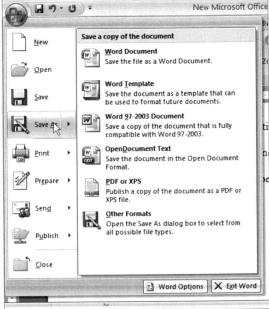

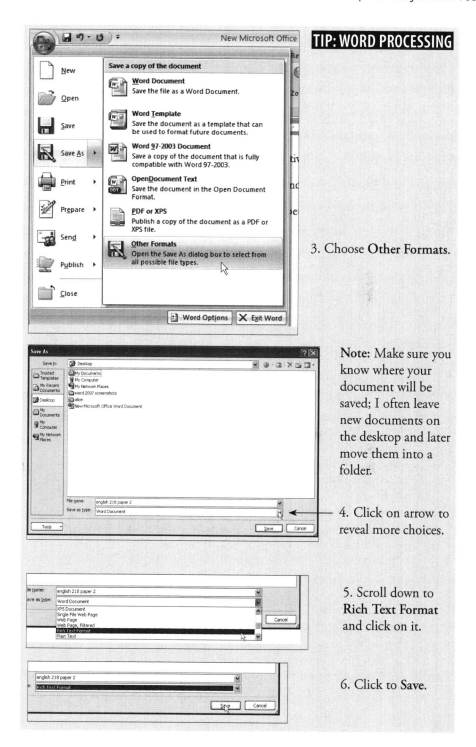

TIP: WORD PROCESSING

3. Choose **Other Formats**.

Note: Make sure you know where your document will be saved; I often leave new documents on the desktop and later move them into a folder.

4. Click on arrow to reveal more choices.

5. Scroll down to **Rich Text Format** and click on it.

6. Click to **Save**.

WRITE A DRAFT

Many writers dislike the sight of a blank page. It can be intimidating, slightly overwhelming. If you have some prewriting and an outline, you have a real advantage. Either way, though, I suggest that you consider starting your draft not with the introduction, but with one of your body paragraphs. Many writers take this approach, with the reasoning that they can't really know how to introduce what they haven't yet written. That may or may not be true; I think the truth lies in what's comfortable for you as well as the specific subject matter you're tackling. The point is that there are no rules for drafting; you should jump around the parts of the paper as much as you want. Once you have all the parts, in draft form, then you can worry about how they go together.

Topic sentences

Like outlines, topic sentences often get no respect. They are viewed as overly simplistic, too obvious. Why should you say what the paragraph is going to be about in the first sentence so plainly? Shouldn't you just let the reader figure it out? No, you shouldn't. And there's nothing simplistic about a well-crafted topic sentence, one that lets the reader know what direction your new paragraph is headed in. Furthermore, even the most accomplished and respected writers use them, as in this example (a single paragraph, taken from the middle of a long article) from *The New Yorker*:

> But, as private colleges became more selective, public colleges became more accommodating. Proportionally, the growth in higher education since 1945 has been overwhelmingly in the public sector. In 1950, there were about 1.14 million students in public colleges and universities and about the same number in private ones. Today, public colleges enroll almost fifteen million students, private colleges fewer than six million.
>
> – Louis Menand, "Live and Learn," *The New Yorker*

The first sentence signals a clear purpose for that paragraph—everything that follows explains, clarifies, supports, and gives examples for the larger idea stated in the topic sentence. Notice also how the final sentence performs a "concluding" function for the paragraph as well.

Good topic sentences make it much easier for your reader to follow your thinking, but they also have an important function for you as the writer: they help ensure that *you* know what you're doing in every single paragraph of your essay. Writing a clear topic sentence forces you to decide what you're trying to accomplish in a given paragraph, and it might also help you eliminate (or move elsewhere) material that doesn't fit with the topic sentence.

REVISE

First drafts are rarely very good. They are a starting point, little more. If you're lucky, you won't have to start over, but you shouldn't rule that out.

What I'm trying to persuade you to do here—for your own benefit—is change your attitude toward revision. If you see revision as the heart of the writing process (which it is, I and a thousand other writers promise you), you might be more willing to do the sometimes difficult work that is ahead of you.

After you finish a draft, you should at least be able to answer two questions:

A COMMON MISCONCEPTION

Revision does not mean to "fix" your draft. It's more than simply finding the errors and correcting them. The word itself, *revise*, has its roots in the idea of sight, and suggests "seeing again." Implied in this is the idea of seeing your work in a new way. First and foremost you want to rethink your ideas—how they connect, how you express them, and so forth.

- What is the big purpose of the paper? (State it in one sentence.)
- What does each body paragraph do to help support or develop the big purpose? (State each paragraph's purpose in a single sentence.)

If you can do those things, it's probably time to let someone else read your paper—then ask that person the same questions. By the way, I'm using the phrase *big purpose* in these questions as a different way of saying thesis.

If you or your reader can't answer those two key questions relatively easily, you have two options:

Option #1: Start over. It sounds awful, but it's often a more efficient use of your time. Sometimes, trying to fix a paper that has major problems (especially problems of purpose and clarity) takes more time than simply starting over. Professional writers do it all the time.

Option #2: Find what *does* work in your draft and start with this material; get rid of everything else.

Here's a simple but important concept my students often miss: If you're not sure what your paper is saying, or why it includes any particular piece of information or evidence, then your reader is going to be more confused than you are.

Revision begins with the awareness that your reader probably has better and more interesting things to do than read your paper. (Okay, if your reader is your professor, then she's getting paid to read it, so she has to—but it might serve you well to imagine some other reader, someone who's paycheck doesn't depend on it.)

Revision through conversation

Another strategy for revision is to imagine your paper as an actual conversation. If you were sitting around with a friend, just talking about this subject, what would both of you be saying? Here's how that conversation might go:

> You: I think that the presence of portable electronic devices in college classrooms has adversely affected the way students and professors interact.
>
> Friend: Hmm.... That's interesting. What makes you think that?
>
> You: Well, for one thing, some professors say that students use these devices to cheat. (This might be a major point within your paper.)
>
> Friend: How do they do that?
>
> You: Well, apparently some students store notes or equations or whatever on their cell phones. (Specific point within body paragraph on cheating.)
> Friend: So why don't colleges just prohibit cell phones?
>
> You: They can do that, but students have also been using iPods—they record themselves saying the notes, then play it back during tests. Most professors just assume the students are listening to music, that maybe it helps them concentrate. (A second specific point in the cheating paragraph.)
>
> Friend: Okay, so cheating is one issue. What's another reason that portable electronic devices have become a problem? (Now he wants another major point/reason.)

You: A lot of people—both students and professors—say they're distracting.

And so on....

If you can imagine a friend who's difficult to persuade, this will help you come up with objections to your arguments. For example, if your friend in this case were particularly contrarian (he likes to be contrary, or take a different view, just because he likes to argue), he might have said, "But what about students who are just listening to music; why should they give that up? Anything a professor can do to help a student relax during a test seems like a good idea to me." Then it would be your job to refute this point.

> **ANTICIPATE THE OPPOSITION**
>
> It might seem like a bad idea to introduce an idea that could contradict your argument, but it can actually make your position stronger. In fact, if you don't deal with obvious objections to your views, your readers often think of those objections, and then they find your argument less persuasive because they believe you can't answer those questions.

PROOFREAD

If you don't proofread your paper, it will most likely contain at least a couple of careless errors. For me, and for many other professors, a paper that seems as if it is the product of a lazy or careless writer is easy to give a low grade to.

Proofreading is actually pretty easy—you're not concerned with the big ideas at this stage, just the correctness of words and sentences. You want the paper to feel polished and professional, so check for spelling errors, missing words, quotation marks turned the wrong direction, anything that might communicate sloppiness to your reader.

I have two specific suggestions that should help you find both careless errors and awkward sentences:

- Read your paper backwards, one sentence at a time (don't read each word backwards). This forces you to focus on each sentence individually and can help you see your writing with fresh eyes.

- Read your paper out loud, or, even better, have someone read it out loud to you. Listen for places where the person has difficulty reading a sentence or finding the right rhythm—that's often a sign that a sentence needs to be rewritten.

Sample student paper

This paper was written by a student in my advanced writing course a few years ago. (See interview with Nichole in Chapter 12, page 199.) This paper is perhaps longer than what many professors will expect in a first-year composition course, but it is a good example of quality research, excellent writing, and solid organization. (I've only included about two-thirds of it here.)

Note: This paper has a few features that some professors may not want you to use in a reserach paper: a personal introduction, interviews, and section headings. Check with your professor before you use any of these in your paper.

Margins: 1 inch on all sides. Indent all paragraphs 1/2 inch. Use the Tab key rather than typing spaces.

Spacing: Double-space all text. (Under *Format* menu, select *Paragraph* and then *Line Spacing*.)

Nichole Reynolds

Professor Cooksey

English 218

5 May 2007

Reynolds 1

Your last name and page number should appear on every page. See pages 40–1 for how to do it.

Title: Don't italicize, underline or bold it.

Out of Alternatives:

Lifestyle Marketing and Myth at Whole Foods

Born in the early 1970's, I only vaguely recall the energy and inflation crises that marked that decade. But, I was deeply marked by the constant and oppressive anxiety that suffused my lower middle class household as a direct result of these national concerns. This tension was agitated by long waits in gasoline queues and evident in the urgent tones that introduced to my young ears adult phrases like inflation, economic policy, and energy consumption. A teenager when my parents filed for bankrupty, I understood their open frustration with President Reagan's fiscal solution to inflation control via increased consumer spending. The insights absorbed from the experiences of my parents largely shaped my adult sensibilities, allowing conscious consumerism to take root as an

---

Reynolds 2

antidote to the rampant consumerism that seemed to have caused their generation such anguish. Now a parent myself, responsible for guiding the values of my own two children, I find that I most frequently exercise my beliefs from the helm of a grocery cart. The example I set through my consumer choices, which are consistently dictated by a deep regard for environment, highlights the importance of making consumer dollars speak to values held dear. I have long assumed that my loyal patronage at Whole Foods Market affirmed my values. However, recent changes in the store's offerings led me to examine more closely what it was that my Whole Foods dollars were saying.

Green Giant ◄——————————————————— This paper uses section headings, which your professor may not allow.

The dollar votes that guide our nation's market economy are "greener" than ever, as recent economic evidence shows a clear trend toward organic foods and sustainable agricultural practices. According to the USDA's Economic Research Service, organic farming "has been one of the fastest growing segments of U.S. agriculture for over a decade," with organic U.S. farmland doubling between the years 2002 and 2005 ("Market-Led Growth"). Organic food is the food market's fastest growing sector, showing a 16.2% increase in sales in 2005 ("Data Set"). Whole Foods Market, the nation's largest natural foods retailer, deserves much credit for the growth of this industry. Rightly applauded for its "core value" philosophy in support of organics and sustainable practices, the company's green-and-white banner has become a beacon for enlightened, eco-friendly shopping. This 27-year-old entity has helped drive a beneficial shift in society's attitudes about organic food and natural products by successfully redefining what was once a marginal hippie movement as a hip and responsible alternative for the

Paper continues on p. 39.

TIP: WORD PROCESSING

Creating a Header with Page Number

Many students have trouble with page numbers and headers. MLA formatting requires that you put your last name and a page number on every page; here's how to do it. If you're using an earlier version of Word, see appendix, page 237.

1. Start by clicking on the **Insert** tab.

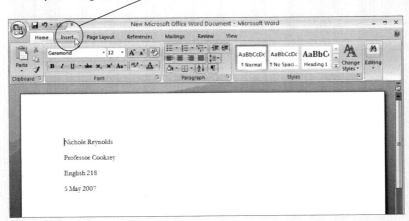

2. Now click on the **Header** icon.

3. Now click on **Page Number**, which will reveal more options. Choose **Insert Page Number**.

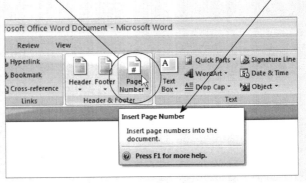

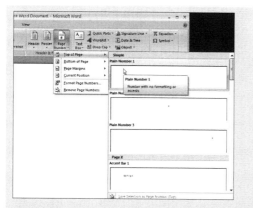

TIP: WORD PROCESSING

3. Choose **Top of Page** and then **Plain Number 1**.

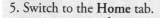

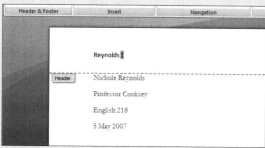

4. Now you're in the header; type your last name and a space before the number.

5. Switch to the **Home** tab.

6. In the **Paragraph** control, choose **Align Text Right**.

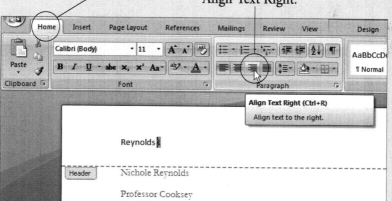

And this is how it should look when you're finished. Simply click somewhere in your text to get out of the header.

globally aware consumer. The company's international presence in 200 locations is evidence of this success, and its dominance in the natural foods arena has gone largely unchallenged until very recently. Statistics indicate an important shift in the mass marketing of organic products as conventional grocers claim a larger share of sales, accounting for 44% of the growth of the total organic food market in 2003 (to natural retailers' 47%) (Dimitri and Oberholtzer 6). The entrance of existing companies into the organic business landscape has weakened Whole Foods' advantageous distinction as *the* source for natural and organic foods.

A number of conventional markets, once content to share a parking lot with Whole Foods, are increasingly eager to share another of its neighbor's features—storefront windows displaying advertisements for their own organic lines. This competition from multiple organic outlets has pressured Whole Foods to consider alternative marketing tactics to ensure long-term viability. Their current approach includes their self-proclaimed status as a lifestyle retailer. In this vein, stores have been transformed into one-stop havens for non-grocery goods such as cruelty-free beauty products, hemp clothing and accessories, micro-brewed beer and global music. Lifestyle is indeed sold as ardently as product: the sum of these material products equals a non-material ethos artfully designed to stroke the discriminating ego. For example, patrons endowed with enough sophistication to value the importance of environmental sustainability and animal rights might reward such morality in the ample wine section or with a selection of fine imported cheese (disregarding, of course, the fossil fuels required to place that Bordeaux or wedge of cheese at a buyer's fingertips). Financial statistics suggest that their campaign of lifestyle promotion is one worth continuing: the company publicly reported record sales and growth for the 2006 fiscal year. Riding

Reynolds 4

this promising growth trajectory, Whole Foods is currently poised to acquire their 110-store strong competitor, Wild Oats Market. But the fact remains that this homegrown company bears the inherent danger of being a business model created in the mold of a new, globalized, consumer-based culture. The same growth credited with raising environmental awareness, supporting local producers, promoting sustainable practices and expanding access to organic goods now threatens to undermine the very principles upon which its success was built.

Whole Checkbook

To visit Whole Foods Market is to become, if briefly, part of a community that embraces what might still be called an alternative code of ethics. It is an overt kind of membership, rife with symbols that herald the values of its members, its natural and organic selection appealing as much to the conscience as to the palate. Stickers on the predominantly fuel efficient cars in the parking lot urge us to 'think globally, shop locally,' and to 'be a local hero, buy locally grown.' Once inside, natural fiber-clad buyers are united under banners proclaiming "Whole Foods, Whole People, Whole Planet," the walls adorned with snippets of eco-conscious "core values" that communicate the company's philosophy. If these gentle mantras still leave the presumed values of a Whole Foods patron unclear, a glance at the cost of produce may help. The 10-30% price premium paid above conventional goods supports a shared sentiment that fostering small, local family farms takes precedence over economic self-interest ("Price Premiums," 73). A commitment to environmental sustainability is evinced in the abundance of reusable shopping bags carried by patrons, and animal rights activists can confidently add cruelty-free personal care products to their cart. Organic food has successfully been marketed as the sun around which all of these sister ideals orbit.

But the value cluster represented through Whole Foods' lifestyle marketing does not have one-size-fits-all appeal; rather, it is clearly targeted at a unique demographic. Michael Pollan, author and trenchant critic of Whole Foods Market's policy, assigns the term "elitist" to organic food. He suggests that "Eating organic has been fixed in the collective imagination as an upper-middle-class luxury, a blue-state affectation as easy to mock as Volvos or lattes." Due to the high price point of most products, many families are indeed priced out of Whole Foods Market. The company acknowledges, in both words and action, the basis for their unflattering moniker "whole checkbook." Heirloom tomatoes, available in season for as little as $2.00 per pound at farmer's markets, sold for as much as $5.98 per pound last season at Whole Foods' location in Hadley, Massachusetts. Anyone familiar with the typical size of this tomato variety understands that at that price, $6.00 frequently buys less than a single fruit. St. Agur blue cheese, a French import, sells for $21.99 per pound at the store's Hadley location. Less than one mile away, down the commercial corridor that was once farmland, competitor Stop & Shop sells the same cheese for four dollars less, at $17.99 per pound. The Whole Foods solution to high prices has not been to simply lower these inflated figures, nor has it been to devise a plan to get more aggressive with local sourcing to lower transport cost—a savings that could be passed along to the consumer. Instead, they have developed a store brand version of most dry goods, effectively disguising early brand-recognition (for the tykes in tow) as genuine concern for the elite checkbook. The emblem for this house brand,

365 Organics, communicates a strong seasonal message and boasts the tagline "everyday value." But, once the euphemisms are stripped away, their store-brand Organic Golden Rounds are no more than gussied up Ritz crackers; their 4-pack kiddie juice boxes more expensive per unit than the 5-pack natural brand that occupies the shelf space beside them. In fact, the two cracker brands are virtually indistinguishable based on nutrition, aside from the fact that—interestingly—the saturated fat content is higher in the organic brand. This crafty solution has allowed Whole Foods to continue to marry the terms "expensive" and "organic," serving the needs of their accurately identified "elite" patrons. However, there is inherent danger in catering to such an educated consumer base. This subset of the populace is versed in the media outlets critical of the gap between the company's contrived public facade and their private business practices. The obvious paradox resulting from this discrepancy is worth exploring in detail.

Fields of Green

Another organic growing pain can be traced to claims on the side of a paper grocery bag at Whole Foods Market. It lists more than ten reasons to buy organic, one of which states that "Buying organic supports small, local family farms." An easy statement to embrace, as it evokes for the virtuous consumer the image of an independent, time-worn farmer in overalls, complete with wheat stalk between sunbaked lips. But this statement is almost as hard to verify as it is easy to accept. As the organic movement is in the infant stages of commodification, consistent national statistics on organic production prove hard to come by. Nationally, California has the most comprehensive system of oversight regarding organic practices, and farm data for 2002 indicated

Reynolds 7

that the largest 3 % of California's organic farms accounted for 55% of the state's total organic sales (Klonsky 249). In this state's case, increased demand for organic products did not result in the widespread success of the small farmer. Considered with the reality of corporate ownership of multiple organic entities, it quickly becomes clear that the pockets lined through the purchase of many of Whole Foods Market's premium priced products are not those of the Vermont dairy farmer of the local fruit grower. Statistics like these suggest that organics are quickly leaving the idealistic sacred ground of alternative movement and stepping onto the battlefield of industry, where success is redefined to accommodate a mass market and longevity is dependent upon adherence to rules of the free market.

As supply struggles to satisfy increasing demand, a latent dysfunction of this success emerges as ever larger food retailers, eager to jump in and grab a piece of the organically grown economic pie, embrace the organic movement. Competition to capitalize on the growing popularity of organic food threatens to compromise the ideals that have long strengthened the foundation of the organic movement. The Cornucopia Institute, a national community-farm watchdog group, warns of the emergence of a breed of "corporate organics" entering the fray with "high production/low-cost" techniques, squeezing out family farms unable to keep pace (Kastel). Capitalist scapegoat WalMart—only briefly in the game but already under fire for organic source integrity—recently began offering organics at their hallmark low, low prices, and conventional supermarket chains like Stop & Shop now carry a store-brand organic line. WalMart is as infamous for making heavy demands on suppliers to feed consumer appetites as Whole Foods is lauded for its well-advertised earth-conscious policies. With WalMart's "corporate

Reynolds 8

organic" presence in the natural foods domain, the two companies will necessarily compete—lifestyle versus product—for potential new patrons. Sustained growth for Whole Foods requires more than just retaining a familiar customer base that anticipates continued commitment to a "core value" philosophy. These new organic patrons, with multiple organic retail choices, may be more concerned with a pocketbook-driven bottom line than with adherence to a philosophy. Satisfying these two opposing forces presents a clear dilemma, one which Whole Foods must navigate with tremendous care. If the company too closely resembles their conventional counterparts (in price or product), elite patrons may seek alternatives; too little and growth is crippled. Under the watchful eye of the environmentally savvy patrons—whom they are partially responsible for educating—the Whole Foods banner proclaiming local, sustainable practices is in danger of shrinking to insignificant proportions. . . .

> I've left out the two sections of Nichole's paper and skipped to the conclusion.

Grassroots

Industrial organics are a double-edged sword, and Whole Foods Market may be growing too large for its philosophical roots to support. But, let's assume that consumer awareness about the organic value cluster represents a trend of the American consumer rather than a fad. It then becomes logical to consider what tenable options to corporate organics exist. One organic faction has been quietly growing, roughly parallel to Whole Foods' timeline. Community Supported Agriculture projects (CSA's) are farms that provide fee-paying members within a community a share of their harvest. The share often includes organically grown seasonal produce, fruits, free range poultry, eggs, and grass fed meats.

Some CSA's even partner with local bakeries and dairies to offer members a more complete range of food items. In 1986, there were 60 CSA's nationwide. Today, that number is 1700, with more than a dozen concentrated here in western Massachusetts. It is important to note that, without exception, the cost of goods for members of a farm share is significantly less than the same goods purchased at a Whole Foods Market. Due to their relative lack of diversity (as compared to a supermarket), CSA's may not pose an immediate challenge to the economic welfare of a company like Whole Foods. But, in truly towing the organic line, these entities have unwittingly established a sort of hierarchy-within-a-hierarchy in the organic domain.

Maureen Dempsey, co-owner of Intervale Farms, a CSA in Westhampton, MA, expresses disgust at the pretense Whole Foods Market has attached to organic foods. Sleek packaging and air-conditioned aisles seem light-years away from Intervale's bucolic landscape, filled with rolling, chemical-free acres, grazing livestock and aging red barns. Maureen's definition of "local" differs vastly from that of Whole Foods, which defines local in terms of hundreds, not tens of miles. She feels that the exorbitant cost of organic produce at Whole Foods Market shamefully misrepresents the movement. To be sure, there is nothing at all "elite" about Maureen's dirt-caked fingernails, industrial-strength rubber farm boots or coarse plaid shirt. Shaking her head, she laments that the way Whole Foods "...does it...is not about the people." Indeed, the differences between corporate standards and a farmer's standards regarding notions of community, local production, and sustainable practices are easy to spot. Whole Foods Market inflates prices, then uses profits to fund community initiatives. In contrast, CSA's have a more direct benefit on communities, by preserving farmland and fostering relationships between community members that move beyond a shopping experience. The locally produced offerings at Whole Foods Market are overshadowed by the more abundant industrial organics, a fact highlighted by the recent E coli scare in California-sourced spinach. CSA's intrinsically uphold the value of locally produced food and, with many allowing hands-on interaction during crop harvest, connect members directly to the source of these "whole foods." The reasonable cost of a farm share welcomes all members of a community, stripping the artificial, elitist pretense from organics. Despite the clear benefits, these entities exist within the broader context of our consumer culture, where advertising is king (an arena in which Whole Foods has proven itself adept). The comparatively limited choices CSA's offer are a significant hurdle for consumers indoctrinated in convenience foods. But, the steady rise of CSA's is evidence that organic roots run deep and can easily support more than one avenue of growth.

The environmental benefits of organic foods, grown without man-made chemicals, are not in question. Rather, the ideology that is the foundation of the organic food movement is targeted in the global crosshairs, raising the question, does a dollar spent at Whole Foods Market simply oil the corporate machine? Their eager embrace of big-business practices has the potential to make them a noticeable weed in the organic garden. Poised on the very edge of mainstream, the company is gambling with their harmonious motto, Whole People, Whole Foods, Whole Planet—it may soon reverberate with more dogma than doctrine.

Reynolds 11

Works Cited

Dempsey, Maureen. Personal interview. 28 Apr. 2007.

Howard, Phil. "Consolidation in Food and Agriculture: Implications for Farmers and Consumers." *California Certified Organic Farmers Magazine* 21.4 (Winter 2003-2004). Web. 28 Mar. 2007.

Kastel, Mark Alan. "Wal-Mart: The Nation's Largest Grocer Rolls Out Organic Products." *Cornucopia Institute*, 2006. Web. 28 Mar. 2007.

Klemperer, Joshua. Personal interview. 26 April 2007.

Klonsky, Karen. "Organic Agricultural Production in California." *California Agriculture: Dimensions and Issues.* Ed. Jerry Siebert. Berkeley, CA: Gianni Foundation. Web. 28 Mar. 2007.

Organic Trade Association. "U.S. Organic Industry Overview." *Organic Trade Association's 2006 Manufacturer's Survey.* Web. 28. Mar. 2007.

"Our Core Values." Whole Foods Market. 20 Feb. 2007. Web. 28 Mar. 2007.

Pollan, Michael. "Mass Natural." *New York Times Magazine* 4 June 2006. Web. 1 May 2007.

"Private Label Products." Whole Foods Market. 2007. Web.15 May 2007.

"Sustainability and Our Future." Whole Foods Market. 2007. Web. 28 Mar. 2007.

U.S. Dept. of Agriculture. Data Set. Economic Research Service. 15 Dec. 2006. 28 Mar. 2007.

U.S. Dept. of Agriculture. "EU and US Market Growth." Economic Research Service. 12 Aug. 2005. Web. 28 Mar. 2007.

U.S. Dept. of Agriculture. "Price Premiums." Economic Research Service. Web. 28. Mar. 2007.

Please see Chapter 11 for in-depth coverage of documentation, including how to format this page.

chapter 4

COMMON ERRORS

Learn the rules, break the rules. In that order.

Correctness is a complicated subject, one that we English teachers don't always agree on. (Old-fashioned English teachers would have corrected the end of that sentence so that it says: ". . . and one *on which* we English teachers don't always agree." The rule not to end a sentence with a preposition was once an absolute one, but then again, so was the rule that declared this to be correct: "He forgat his book.")

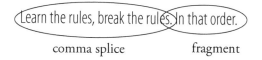

comma splice   fragment

Those are both errors, and yet I doubt you had any difficulty reading the sentences or understanding my meaning. In fact, I think that both "errors" could be justified because they allow me to deliver my meaning with some style. Written "correctly," they would be revised like this:

> Learn the rules, and then break the rules. You should do it in that order.

But now there's a new error: I say to do *it* in that order—but the *it* refers to two things, learning the rules and breaking the rules. So here's the new revision:

> Learn the rules, and then break the rules. You should do those things in that order.

Now, it's entirely correct grammatically. But it sounds awful.

In terms of correctness, you have two goals that are often in conflict—you want your writing to be grammatically correct (if it's not, some readers won't take you seriously), but you also want it to sound good.

This chapter shows you some of the most common rules writers need to know. As for breaking them, I offer two guidelines: Know that you're doing it, and do it for a good reason.

How this chapter is organized:

> **Commonly confused words**
>
> **Sentence construction**
>
> **Sentence errors**
>
> **A few rules worth learning: apostrophes/possession, commas, titles, capitalization**

COMMONLY CONFUSED WORDS

4.1   accept / except

> Please **accept** my gift of $14,000 so you can buy a car.
>
> Any car is fine, **except** a purple one.

✓ 4.2   all right (not alright)

> Even though you see it all the time, there is no such word as *alright*. It's all wrong, all the time. (Don't feel bad if you didn't know this—I was on my way to earning a second master's degree before I learned it.)
>
> The man left the emergency room when he decided he felt all right.
>
> Note: You should also know that *all right* is informal—you probably shouldn't use it in academic writing.

4.3   a lot (not alot)

A lot of people went to see the artist's video of David Beckham sleeping.

Alot is not correct—don't use it. Also, you should know that while it is correct, *a lot* is informal; in academic writing, it would be better to express a large number more precisely: More than 2,000 visitors saw the artist's video in the exhibition's first week.

4.4   a part / apart

He is **a part** of the oldest club on campus.

(He *belongs* to it.)

Apart from her car insurance, she paid all her bills without her parents' help.

(That one expense is *separate from* the others.)

✓ 4.5   effect / affect

Effect is (almost always) a noun:

Moving out of his parents' house had at least one positive **effect**: It forced him to get a job.

Affect is (almost always) a verb:

Moving out of his parents' house negatively **affected** his bank statement.

A complication you will only rarely encounter: Effect can also be a verb. In that case, it means *to bring about, or to cause to occur*.

The Board of Education hopes to **effect** change on a system-wide basis.

4.6   imply / infer

The speaker **implied** that college freshmen were irresponsible.

(Speakers and writers imply things.)

We **inferred** from the speaker's comments that he believed college freshmen to be irresponsible.

(Listeners and readers infer—or come to a conclusion about something—based on what they hear and read.)

4.7   it's / its   never **its'**

It's is a contraction (the apostrophe shows that a letter has been "contracted," or taken away) and always means one of two things: *It is* or *It has.*

It's been raining all day. (It has been raining all day.)
It's going to be a long day. (It is going to be a long day.)

Its is always possessive:

The dog wagged its tail.

(If you wrote **it's** by accident, the sentence would say: The dog wagged it is tail.) See pages 67–9 for possession rules.

4.8   lose / loose

If you keep playing like that, you're going to **lose** the game.
When the bolts came **loose**, the wheel spun off the axle.

4.9   then / than

Then shows when something happened:

> We ate breakfast, and **then** we went hiking.

Than makes a comparison:

> Stewie's argument was more persuasive **than** Brian's.

4.10   there / their / they're

There shows location:

> He put the clothes over **there**.

Their shows possession ("ownership"):

> That is **their** house.

They're is a contraction of *they are*:

> **They're** not going to be home.

4.11   to / too

To is a preposition and an "infinitive":

> I'm going **to** the game. He's planning **to** quit.

Too is an "intensifier":

> He has **too** much rice. I was **too** tired to go.

4.12   who / which / that

Those are the students **who** wrote the editorial.

(Don't use *that* when you refer to people. Many writers would have written, *Those are the students that wrote the editorial*, which would be wrong.)

Here are the papers **that** need to be revised.

(You can also use *which* in this example, but most American grammarians recommend *that*.)

The revised papers, **which** I've attached to this e-mail, are ready for your comments.

(This one should be *which*. A simple guideline: If you have a construction like this and you're trying to decide between *that* and *which*, use *that* if there's no comma, and *which* if there is. See also pages 70–1 or do a Google search for restrictive versus nonrestrictive clauses.)

4.13   Who's / whose

Who's the man with the crooked hat?

(Contraction of **Who is** . . . .)

That's the man **whose** hat is crooked.

(Possession: the hat belongs to the man.)

4.14   would have or would've (not would of)

Writers make this mistake for a good reason—because they write what they hear, or what they say.

His argument **would have** been more persuasive if he had included better evidence.

Note: In formal writing, it's best to avoid contractions. If the writing is informal, it might be acceptable to write **would've**.

4.15   you and I vs. you and me (and other related errors)

Whenever you hear "That's between she and I," the speaker has made a grammatical mistake, and it's one that you should learn how to avoid in your writing. Grammar people call it an example of "hyper-correction," meaning that the person who says something like "between she and I" believes he's being extra conscientious, grammatically speaking. He remembers being corrected by English teachers when he said things like, "Me and Josh are going to the movie." The teacher would have said, sternly, "You mean, *Josh and I* are going to the movie." And the teacher would be right because *Josh and I* are a subject (they're doing something), not an object (having something done to them, or receiving an action). So if you said, "The teacher hates me and Josh," you'd be correct, because in that case *me and Josh* are objects—they are receiving the teacher's hatred (or what they imagine to be her hatred; she was probably just trying to help).

Let's look at some examples.

subject   object

Sally loves Hank.

When you introduce another person being loved, that's when things get complicated—both in love and grammar. I should say, it gets complicated when the other person is a pronoun: **I / me** instead of Fred, **she / her** instead of Wanda, etc.

Sally loves Hank and (**I or me?**).

The trick is to mentally remove *Hank and*; then it's easy to see the right choice. Think of it this way: You'd never be tempted to say, *Sally loves I*, right? So why would you be tempted to say, *Sally loves Hank and I*?

YES   Sally loves Hank and **me**.

Now let's change Hank to a pronoun too. Is it *he* or *him*? Same principle: You wouldn't say, *Sally loves he.* You'd say, *Sally loves him.* So:

YES Sally loves both him and me.

Believe it or not, that's correct. It should *not* be, *Sally loves both he and I.* Never ever ever. No matter how many times you hear people on TV say it—it's not right, and educated people know the difference.

Note: If you're bothered by how your sentence sounds when you write it correctly, consider changing things around. Instead of saying, Tom sent an invitation to Betsy and me (*not* Betsy and I), you could reverse the order: *When Betsy and I received Tom's invitation, we hoped we would be out of town that weekend.*

When you use a preposition (*between* in this example), the same rules apply:

NO That is between he and I.

YES That is between him and me.

THE IMPORTANCE OF *SOUND*

Sound does matter in language, both in writing and speaking; when the grammatically correct way of writing something results in a sentence that sounds wrong, try to rewrite it. Often this means changing a sequence of two or three sentences, rather than just a word or two.

4.16   your / you're

Your shows possession:

Your hat is crooked. **Your** beliefs are ridiculous.

(The second example is abstract. See Abstract Possession later in this chapter.)

You're is a contraction of you are:

If you don't leave now, **you're** going to be late.

SENTENCE CONSTRUCTION

If you've never understood "grammar," don't worry. I'll keep this simple.

First, an analogy. Think of writing as being like a house. You, the writer, are like the architect who designs the house. (You're also the general contractor, the electrician, the painter, etc., but we'll keep the analogy simple for now.) When it comes to grammar, you're more like an engineer than an architect.

Engineers are the ones who decide if a house is going to work, structurally. When the architect designs a balcony that hangs thirty feet over the back wall of the house, it's the engineer who would say, "That's not going to work." The engineer is less concerned with how the house is going to look, and much more concerned with whether or not the it's going to stand up and all of its parts are going to "work."

That's how you need to think about sentences.

We're not talking about what would look interesting. We're talking about whether or not the thing "works"—because if you have a paper full of flawed sentences, it's like a house where the walls are in the wrong places, or built from the wrong materials. It might look like a house, but it won't be safe. Now apply that analogy to a paper with numerous sentence errors: It might look like a paper, but it won't really make a lot of sense, and it might even fail in its most basic mission—to communicate with a reader.

Let's start with the "basic materials" of a sentence.

Independent clause

The independent clause is simply a subject and a verb, like this:

> Jim drove.

It may seem strange, but that's a complete sentence. It's grammatically correct. It doesn't say much, but remember that we're not interested in how much meaning the sentence has (that's the architect's job)—we're only interested in whether or not it functions grammatically.

Add another subject (and Tina), an object (their car), and a prepositional phrase (into a bank lobby)—and then you have something that looks like a more typical sentence.

> Jim and Tina drove their car into a bank lobby.

That's simple, and obviously a correct sentence. But you can't write a paper full of sentences like that—it would be like building a house where each room had a single window and a doorway. Too basic.

So you want to add another idea:

> No one got hurt.

If you try to put those two thoughts together (without connecting them), you have a problem:

> Jim and Tina drove their car into a bank lobby no one got hurt.

You know that's not right. (That, by the way, is called a **run-on**.)

You could simply put a period between the two parts. That would make it grammatically correct, but it wouldn't read very well. Again, too basic.

The natural thing to do would be to connect the two parts, and that's where you need a coordinating conjunction.

Coordinating conjunctions (the important ones)

and   **but**   **or**   **so**

> The others are **for, nor, yet.** These aren't used frequently in contemporary writing.

How to "coordinate" two parts of a sentence: Put a comma at the end of the first complete thought, add the coordinating conjunction, and then write the second complete thought:

> Jim and Tina drove their car into a bank lobby, **but** no one got hurt.

Now the two independent clauses have been joined together in a way that is grammatically correct.

For some fun retro-grammar, go to youtube.com and search for *conjunction junction*. These cartoons from the 1970s are pure genius. Other cartoons from Schoolhouse Rock include interjections, nouns, etc. Yes, they were created for kids—it's how I learned my parts of speech—but plenty of adults still love them.

Finally, some of you may know the coordinating conjunctions as FANBOYS (for, and, not, but, or, yet, so)—it's an easy way to remember them all.

Dependent words and clauses

Another way to connect two complete thoughts is to make one of those thoughts "dependent" on the other. You do that by using a dependent word at the beginning of the complete thought; this turns what would be an independent clause into a dependent one:

> Even though Jim and Tina drove their car into a bank lobby.

Starting with a dependent word (or words, in this case: even though) changes the grammar of that clause. Without *even though*, it's a complete thought; with it, it's not. This type of sentence error is called a **fragment**. The clause is no longer independent—it can't stand alone. It *depends on* something else. The something else is an independent clause. If we add one, the entire new sentence will be complete:

> Even though Jim and Tina drove their car into a bank lobby, no one got hurt.

You can also reverse the order, putting the dependent clause later in the sentence:

> No one got hurt when Jim and Tina drove their car into a bank lobby.

In this construction, you don't need the comma between the two elements.

MOST COMMON DEPENDENT WORDS

after	due to	so that
although	even if	until
as	even though	when
as if	how	whenever
as though	if	whereas
because	if only	while
before	since	

COMMON SENTENCE ERRORS

4.17   Run-on / comma splice

A run-on sentence has more than one complete thought in it; it becomes a run-on when you don't connect—or separate—those thoughts grammatically.

> Jim drove his car into a pile of snow he could not get the car back onto the road.

In that "sentence," there are two complete thoughts; the first one ends after snow. That's a pretty obvious error, and not one that many students would make. But this version of the same mistake is less obvious:

> Jim drove his car into a pile of snow **then** he could not get the car back onto the road.

This sounds better, but it's still a run-on, because **then** doesn't have the grammatical power to connect the two complete thoughts.

Note: A comma splice has essentially the same problem as a run-on, but it has a comma between the two complete thoughts—which still isn't enough to connect the parts.

> Jim drove his car into a pile of snow, he could not get the car back onto the road.

Run-ons and comma splices can be corrected in two basic ways—either by separating the complete thoughts (with a period or semicolon), or by connecting them (with a variety of methods).

Separating with a period—acceptable but often simplistic

> Jim drove his car into a pile of snow. He could not get the car back onto the road.

Connecting —a better solution

With a coordinating conjunction:

> Jim drove his car into a pile of snow, **and** he could not get the car back onto the road.

With a dependent word:

> **After** Jim drove his car into a pile of snow, he could not get the car back onto the road.

Or with a dependent word, reversing the parts (and changing a pronoun):

> Jim could not get his car back onto the road **after** he drove it into a pile of snow.

4.18   Fragment

A fragment is an incomplete sentence. It can happen for a variety of reasons, most often because you've made one part of the sentence dependent—without giving it another part that's independent to balance it, like this:

> When there is no more gas left and cheaper sources of fuel can't be found.

It's that first word, "when," that makes the sentence a fragment—because it's a dependent word in this case. Like most fragments, the sentence leaves the reader hanging, waiting for something else. The thing you're waiting for is the independent clause, the thing that will make the sentence complete:

> When there is no more gas left and cheaper sources of fuel can't be found, more research will be devoted to alternative energies.

The key to this is the part that comes after the comma—that's the independent clause (the part that can stand by itself).

A complication you'll enjoy . . .

Fragments aren't always a mistake. Experienced writers use them for good effect—they can break up the rhythm of your sentences and provide emphasis. In the quotation that opened this chapter, for example, I used a fragment ("In that order.") to call attention to the fact that writers should learn the rules *first*.

Purposeful fragments can help balance long sentences and provide a quick punch of information. But use them sparingly—too many fragmented sentences (even when written intentionally) will look gimicky, and they will lose the power to grab the reader's attention.

4.19   Subject-verb agreement

Subjects and verbs have to agree "in number," which means that a singular subject takes a singular verb (It falls), and a plural subject takes a plural verb (They fall). This is usually pretty obvious; not many of you would write this:

> The paper go into that drawer.

That's obviously incorrect. It should be:

> The paper goes into that drawer.

4.20   Compound subject (subject-verb agreement)

When you have a two-part subject joined by *and*, you need a plural verb:

> The chair and the table **are** in the truck.

Some writers are thrown off by the fact that table (which is singular) is right next to the verb, which might make them choose *is* for the verb instead of *are*. But *are* is correct because chair and table, together, become plural.

When you have a two-part subject joined by *or*, you choose the verb based on the subject closest to the verb.

Singular

> The plumber or his assistant **does** a final inspection of the work.

Plural

> The plumber or his assistants **do** a final inspection of the work.

4.21   There is / There are (subject-verb agreement)

When you start a sentence with one of these constructions, you have to choose the right verb (*is* or *are*) based on the subject that comes next.

There *is* one way to get rid of fleas on your dog.
There *are* many ways your dog can get fleas.

In the first sentence, the subject is *way*, which is singular.
In the second sentence, the subject is *ways*, which is plural.

Note: Starting a sentence with *There is* or *There are* is weak—try to rewrite your sentence to avoid this construction. (See Chapter 5: Editing.)

4.22   –ing subject (subject-verb agreement)

When your subject is an –ing word (also called a *gerund*) as a subject, you need a singular verb.

Singular

According to Smith and Fleisher, taking courses in these fields ~~are~~ **is** less attractive to students who are concerned about their GPAs.

4.23   Interruptions (subject-verb agreement)

In English, we tend to like the subject and verb right next to each other, but sometimes we want to separate them, as in this example:

The Abominable Snowman, though never found by any of the researchers, lives on in myth.

Some writers might have been tempted to think that the plural noun *researchers* would make the next verb *live* instead of *lives*. But if you remove the "interruption" (all of the information inside the two commas), it's easy to see that *Abominable Snowman* is the subject and that *lives* is the right verb.

4.24 Pronoun reference errors

These errors usually occur when you have a singular (meaning one) subject that you mistakenly connect to a plural (more than one) pronoun.

Singular   Plural

Incorrect   **Each student** must submit **their** financial aid form by Friday at 5 p.m.

Four possible solutions:

Each student must submit his or her financial aid form by Friday at 5 p.m.

Students must submit their financial aid forms by Friday at 5 p.m

You must submit your financial aid form by Friday at 5 p.m.

Financial aid forms must be submitted by Friday at 5 p.m.

4.25 Faulty parallelism

Parallelism means that two or more elements are consistent with each other.

Parallel   Not parallel

The college's student government was responsible for **recruiting new members**, **submitting a budget**, and ~~enforcement of all policies.~~
enforcing all policies.

The first two responsibilities are parallel to each other, because they both begin with an -ing verb and then follow with a noun. The third responsibility, in order to be parallel, must also start with an -ing verb (enforcing) and follow with a noun.

Here's an example from (everyone's favorite!) Wikipedia:

Find something that can be improved and make it better—for example, spelling, grammar, rewriting for readability, adding content, or removing non-constructive edits.

Fix it and send me (and Wikipedia) your revision.

A FEW RULES WORTH LEARNING

I've always believed that English teachers rely too much on rules—and that students learn to write more clearly as a result of reading and practice. Still, you'll avoid a lot of mistakes if you refer to these guidelines for apostrophes, commas, titles, and capitalization.

Apostrophes for contractions

A contraction means that something becomes smaller. With words, contractions are formed with apostrophes, like this:

is not = isn't

The apostrophe here shows that a letter has been removed. The principle is the same even if the apostrophe replaces more letters, as in these words:

would have = would've

he will = he'll

Apostrophes for possession

When we speak, we create the "sound" of possession by adding an *s* sound. But when we write, we use an apostrophe. And it needs to go in the right place.

If you learn three basic rules, you'll get your apostrophe in the right place 90 percent of the time.

Rule #1: Don't add apostrophes to words that are simply plurals.

Five cars were left in the parking lot overnight.

Nothing "belongs" to the cars in this case, so there's no apostrophe.

ABSTRACT POSSESSION

Often, the idea of possession is obvious: Something "belongs" to someone: Jim's hat, or Tina's car.

But there's another form of "possession" that is less obvious—mainly because it isn't physical. I call it abstract, or conceptual, possession. For example:

> Mike's anger caused him to lose his job.

Does Mike "possess" his anger? Not in any physical sense—but in a grammatical sense, yes.

The most common form of abstract possession is emotional: Mike's anger, Tina's love of her children, Paul's fear of dogs, etc.

But other types of possession are even harder to detect because they involve what I'll call an "abstract state of being."

> Mike's inability to control his anger caused him to lose his job.

Again, it's hard to think of "inability" as belonging to Mike, but it does.

Rule #2: In most cases, just add 's to the word doing the possessing:

> One car's trunk had been broken into.

(The trunk "belongs to"—or is a part of—the car, so you add 's to car.)

> The cat's paw got caught in the door.

(One cat "possesses" a paw that got caught in the door.)

The rule is the same if the person/animal/thing doing the possessing ends with the letter s:

> James's paw got caught in the door.

Also, it doesn't matter if the cat had gotten two paws stuck in the door—the possession rule would be the same:

The cat's paws got caught in the door.

Okay, it probably matters to the cat, but it doesn't matter to us, at least not grammatically.

Rule #3: When more than one person or thing is doing the possessing, the apostrophe usually goes after the s.

Five cars were left in the parking lot overnight. All the cars' windshields were smashed.

Note the difference between "Five cars" (in Rule #1), where there's no possession, and "the cars' windshields," where the windshields "belong" to the cars. Also remember that it wouldn't matter if there were an adjective in there too: "the cars' *dirty* windshields."

Rule #4: Possession with plural words like men, women, etc.

The plural form of most words ends with an s: tables, chairs, elephants, houses, trees, and so on. But some words—like *women, people, men*—form a plural without the final s. When the plural form of a word does not end in **s**, add **'s**.

The women's room is down the hall, on your left.

(The room that "belongs to" women is down the hall.)

Commas

Six rules cover just about every use of the comma. Here they are:

After introductory material

After the judge's recess, the plaintiff disappeared.
Nonetheless, all the cars were ticketed.

Around an "interruption"

James, the oldest boy in the class, was also the tallest.

With items in a list or series

The recipe calls for apples, pears, peaches, and cinammon.

(Note: The comma after the next-to-last item in the list—*peaches*, in this case—is the subject of great controversy among grammar geeks. Some consider it optional, while others insist it must be included. If you're curious, google *Oxford comma*.)

Between two complete thoughts, with a conjunction

The police officer arrested the student protesters, but a judge later ruled that the officer had used excessive force.

With many uses of *which* (aka nonrestrictive clauses)

Her favorite food was artichokes, which he found repulsive.

I explain the grammatical rule in the next few examples, but it may be just as helpful for you to simply listen for the slight pause that usually occurs with these constructions.

When to use *that* versus *which* can be confusing, particularly when you're trying to determine whether or not you need a comma; grammatically, the key is to know whether you're dealing with a restrictive or a nonrestrictive clause:

Cell phones that ring during movies are extremely annoying.

Here, the meaning of cell phones is *restricted*—the sentence says that in *one specific circumstance* (during a movie) cell phones are annoying. No comma is needed.

> Cell phones, which became widely available in the mid-90s, can be extremely useful.

Here, the meaning is *not* restricted—the sentence says that cell phones can be extremely useful. The other piece of information is not essential to the meaning of the sentence. (Yes, this example is very similar to the "interruption" rule.)

With quotations (see also Chapter 7)

> Red Barber once said, "Baseball is dull only to dull minds."

Note: If the quote flows grammatically within the sentence, then the comma is usually omitted:

> Red Barber once described baseball as being dull "only to dull minds."

Titles

Generally, titles of shorter works go inside quotation marks; titles of longer works are italicized.

Quotation marks

Article in a newspaper, magazine, or academic journal:
David Carr's "A Guide to Smartphone Manners"
Essay in a book: Philip Lopate's "Portrait of My Body"
Short story: Alice Munro's "Boys and Girls"
Poem: Seamus Heaney's "Digging"
Episode of a TV show: "Put the Dog Out" (episode of *Family Guy*)
Song: Sex Pistols' "Anarchy in the U.K."

Italics

Book: Herman Melville's *Moby Dick*
Collection of essays, stories, or poems:
    Seamus Heaney's *Collected Poems:1965-1975*
Textbook: *Quick and Dirty: A Compact Guide to Writing, Reading, and Research*
Album: Neutral Milk Hotel's *In the Aeroplane Over the Sea*
Movie: *Lost in Translation*
Television show: *Family Guy*

Complication: Sometimes, particularly with poets, fiction writers, and essayists, the name of a book will also be the name of a story, poem, or essay within the book. For example, Seamus Heaney's first collection of poems was called *Death of a Naturalist*. So, when referring to the book as a whole, I would italicize the title. However, there's also a poem by the same name in the book; when I refer to that poem, I would use quotes: "Death of a Naturalist."

The title of *your* paper

Capitalize the first and last words (always, no exceptions) and all other words, with the following exceptions:

    articles: a, an, the
    prepositions (even long ones): of, on, to, for, with, about, through (and many others)
    conjunctions: and, but, or, so, yet, nor, for
    infinitive: to

Example:

    An Analysis of Symbiotic Relationships among Birds, Bees, and Flies

Generally, you capitalize all the "important" words.

Also, when you put a title on your own paper, don't do anything to it—no quotation marks, no italics, no bold. Nothing. The only exception to this is if you have a quote within your title, like this:

    Landscape, Memory, and Myth in Heaney's "Personal Helicon"

Capitalization

People's names

Ernest Hemingway, Fred Flintstone (it doesn't matter that he's a cartoon character—it's still his name)

Places

Paris, France; Wheeling, West Virginia; North Carolina's Outer Banks

Complication: Some "places" don't get capitalized: southern Virginia (because there is no place by that name), eastern Massachusetts

However, you do capitalize regions in some cases (but not compass directions):

> He is thinking about going to college in the South.
> To get to the bank, you drive south towards Atholl.
> Many people died when the West was settled.
> Chicopee is west of Worcester.

When the compass direction (north, south, east, west, northeast, southwest, etc.) becomes a "place," you should capitalize it. When it simply tells which direction something is in, you don't.

Languages / people / cuisines

English, French, Chinese, Russian, Portuguese, etc.

Organizations / institutions

Congress, the Department of Labor, Seattle Central Community College, United Auto Workers (because it's the formal name of a union)

Brand names

Kleenex, Apple (the computer), Panasonic, Tide (laundry detergent)

Professional titles / academic titles

Typically, if someone's title comes before his or her name, you capitalize it; if it comes after, you don't:

> I met with Vice President Bausch for almost an hour last week.

> The meeting was led by Robert Bausch, a vice president at the college.

Additional resources

To learn more about grammar and other issues of correctness, I recommend the site at Purdue University; do a google search for *owl purdue grammar*.

chapter 5

EDITING

*The difference between the right word and the almost right word
is the difference between lightning and the lightning bug.*
~ Mark Twain

Editing is the last thing you should do before you turn your paper in. Make sure you leave yourself some time for this step—it can make a big difference in how "polished" your paper feels, and therefore also what kind of grade it gets.

Some suggestions about how to approach editing

- Always work from a printed copy of your paper—it's easier to see errors that way.

- Read your paper out loud, slowly.

- Read your paper backwards, one sentence at a time. This is useful because it disrupts your usual flow and forces you to focus on each sentence individually.

- Ask a friend to read it and mark obvious problems. If your friend is a good writer, ask her to make other sentence-level suggestions too. (Remember, though, that this is not the time to worry about the quality of the "big" ideas—just focus on words and sentences.)

If you really want to find out whether or not your paper reads well, have a friend read it out loud to you. Listen for places where she has trouble reading a sentence—these can indicate problems with rhythm and emphasis.

You have three jobs when you edit (in order of importance)

1. Find and correct obvious errors
2. Cut useless words and phrases
3. Rewrite sentences to improve clarity, rhythm and readability
   (See also Chapter 6: Sentence Sophistication)

FIND AND CORRECT OBVIOUS ERRORS

See Chapter 4 for many common errors that you should be able to correct in editing. Make sure, for example, that you have not misspelled anyone's name (especially your professor's in the heading). When you refer to Jane Smiley as "Jane Smily," your professor will doubt your ability to pay close attention to details.

 Spell Check is useful, of course, but it doesn't replace common sense. For example, if you misspell *definitely* (as many people do), Spell Check will frequently offer *defiantly* as the first option to correct your error. But this is an entirely different word, with a very different meaning. If you blindly accept every suggestion Spell Check makes without thinking about the word, you're likely to end up with some ridiculous mistakes. As always, think for yourself.

CUT USELESS WORDS AND PHRASES

I believe more in the scissors than I do in the pencil.
~ Truman Capote

I know, you're trying to get *up* to your professor's minimum length requirement. She said you have to have a five-page paper, and you've just barely got five. And now I'm telling you to cut words. But it's worth it—professors appreciate crisply written prose that doesn't include wasted words. (I should, for example, change the end of that sentence to this: doesn't waste words.) As long as you're in the ballpark for length requirements, most professors won't mind if you come up a little short (though it never hurts to check with them on this point). When I ask for a 1000-word essay, I would much rather read—and always give a higher grade to—the paper that has 950 tight words, not the one that has 1000 words but is full of bloated phrases.

"I" STATEMENTS / FIRST PERSON: PROCEED WITH CAUTION

I think / I believe / It is my opinion / The point I am making is

Using the first person in an academic paper is a controversial issue, so I offer a brief description of the two approaches. Check with your professor for guidance.

Many professors don't allow students to use first person . . . for two reasons: first, they claim that students who rely on "I think" (and its variants) leads them to make personal claims rather than clearly reasoned points; second, many professors argue that the first person simply isn't necessary, as in this case:

> I believe that George Will's definition of reality television is too narrow, and that he ignores many compelling and worthwhile programs that use the "reality" format.

Simply eliminating the first person results in a more efficient sentence that doesn't lose any clarity:

> George Will's definition of reality television is too narrow, and he ignores many compelling and worthwhile programs that use the "reality" format.

But other professors . . . are encouraging their students to use first person ("I") in some circumstances; they argue that it's good for students to use these constructions as a way of making clear (both for themselves as writers and for readers) what they are saying, and as a way of differentiating this from what their sources are saying. For example, let's say that you've just paraphrased an assertion from one of your sources:

> George Will characterizes the emergence of reality television as the end of Western civilization.

Now, let's say that you disagree with this, and you're going to say so in your next sentence. Using an "I" statement can alert your reader that he needs to shift gears and be ready to encounter your view:

> **I would argue**, however, that Will's definition of reality television is too narrow, and that he ignores many compelling and worthwhile programs that use the "reality" format.

(The transitional word *however* also helps the reader make the shift.)

Useless words

Inexperienced writers often use a lot of words and phrases that don't add anything to their sentences. They're filler—get rid of them. (The worst offenders are the first five, in bold.)

really	for all intents and purposes
very	particular
basically	in the process of
actually	more or less
kind of	for the most part
sort of	all things considered
generally	in a manner of speaking
individual	as a matter of fact
specific	definitely
type of	as it were

There are many ways to say *because*, but none of them really says anything that *because* doesn't say. Less sophisticated readers may be impressed by these phrases, but your professors won't be. Replace them with *because*.

the reason for	on account of
for the reason that	considering the fact that
due to the fact that	on the grounds that
in light of the fact that	because of the fact that

More words that can replace phrases

when	on the occasion of
	in a situation in which
	under circumstances in which
about	as regards
	in reference to
	with regard to
	concerning the matter of
	where _____ is concerned

now / today	at this point in time
	at the present time
	in this day and age

must / should	it is crucial that
	it is necessary that
	there is a need/necessity for
	it is important that

can	is able to
	has the opportunity to
	has the capacity for
	has the ability to

may / might	it is possible that
	there is a chance that
	it could happen that
	the possibility exists for

REWRITE FOR CLARITY

It / this / things: vague language

My colleague Elizabeth Trobaugh doesn't allow the word *this* in student papers. Her opposition to the word is well-reasoned: Students are often unclear what words like *it* and *this* refer to. Or they have a vague idea but don't take the time to spell it out. Here's a sequence of sentences from a recent student paper:

> So maybe other cultures have **things** we don't. Sometimes they are heavily valued, other times not so much. In **this** case **it** is.

In *which* case *what* is? Be specific. As a writer, your job is to make it as easy as possible for the reader to understand what you have to say. (I can't even offer you a revised version of that sentence because I don't know what, exactly, the writer was trying to say.)

Here's an example of one I can revise:

> Technology enhances the way we live our lives and makes everything about it more efficient.

This is actually a grammatical error (because *it*, which is singular, refers to *lives*, which is plural) rather than a problem of vagueness. Revised (for wordiness and grammar):

> Technology enhances our lives and makes everything about **them** more efficient.

> Or, even more simply: Technology enhances our lives and makes us more efficient.

Another example, from a student essay about obesity in America:

> David Zinczenko grew up with a "daily choice between McDonalds, Taco Bell, and Kentucky Fried Chicken." He believes that **it** isn't the eater's fault. **It's** the issue that fast food restaurants are everywhere and Americans have no choice, but to eat **it**.

Revised:

> David Zinczenko grew up with a "daily choice between McDonalds, Taco Bell, and Kentucky Fried Chicken." He believes that **teen obesity** isn't the eater's fault. Because fast food restaurants are everywhere, Americans have no choice but to eat **unhealthy foods**.

There is / There are

These constructions are a poor way to begin a sentence—they tend to be weak because they allow you to avoid saying anything about your subject. For example:

> There is a reason why good writers avoid empty phrases.

What's the reason? Why not tell me in the same sentence?

Revised:

Good writers avoid empty phrases because readers resent being forced to read unnecessary words.

"To be" verbs

One of my high school teachers made us write an entire paper without using any "to be" verbs. In other words, we couldn't use *am, is, was, were, are, been, being,* or *be*. It's difficult not to use these verb forms because they're the most common verbs in the English language. (In that sentence, I used two: It *is* difficult, and they *are* the most common....)

I wouldn't suggest that you try to eliminate *all* of these verbs in your writing, but it can be helpful to replace as many of them as possible with stonger, more expressive verbs.

Here's an example, using my sentence from above:

> It's difficult not to use these verb forms because ....

As I thought about how to get rid of that first *is*, I couldn't just think of a synonym for *is difficult*. I had to think about the entire concept and try to express it differently. Here's what I came up with, and it's no accident that I think the revision is superior:

> We rely on these verb forms because ....

Or, if you didn't want to use *We* :

> Writers rely on these verb forms because ....

TRANSITIONS

Between paragraphs

You've probably heard that you're supposed to have transitions between paragraphs, but what does that mean exactly? In short, it means that there's a link between the ideas in one paragraph and the ideas in the next.

The example below shows the final sentence of a paragraph about low wages for Wal-Mart employees, and then the next paragraph, which focuses on the lack of health insurance options for those employees.

> ... It is the greed of the management of this company that keeps their workers earning below poverty wages.

> Many of the employees at Wal-Mart are unable to get an adequate health plan for themselves and their families due to costly health care costs. . . .

The original has no transition between the two paragraphs, but it's pretty easy to create a link between those ideas. The simplest way to do it is to use an idea from the last sentence of the first paragraph, briefly, in the first sentence of the next paragraph.

> . . . It is the greed of the management of this company that keeps their workers earning below poverty wages.
> Low wages are only part of the problem, though, because many Wal-Mart employees are unable to get an adequate health plan for themselves and their families due to costly health care costs. . . .

A different version, one that makes a closer connection between the two issues:

> . . . It is the greed of the management of this company that keeps their workers earning below poverty wages.
> With such low wages, most Wal-Mart employees are also effectively cut off from adequate health care for themselves and their families. . . .

Between sentences

Many writers assume that transitions are only for paragraphs, but you need them between (and often within) sentences too.

> Wal-Mart's health insurance covers only 50.2 percent of their 1.4 million U.S. employees. The industry average is 65 percent of workers insured.

The key to making a good transition between these two sentences is to think about how the ideas relate to one another. These ideas are in contrast, so you want a transitional word or phrase that shows that contrast:

> Wal-Mart's health insurance covers only 50.2 percent of their 1.4 million U.S. employees **whereas** the industry average is 65 percent.

TRANSITIONAL WORDS / PHRASES

SIMILARITY	CONTRAST	CAUSE AND EFFECT
likewise	but	accordingly
similarly	however	consequently
also	in contrast	hence
too	on the other hand	so
just as . . .	whereas	thus
	on the contrary	therefore
	nevertheless	
	still	
	yet	

EXAMPLE	ADDITIONAL SUPPORT	EMPHASIS
for example	additionally	certainly
for instance	again	even
namely	also	indeed
specifically	and	in fact
to illustrate	as well	of course
	equally important	truly
	further	
	furthermore	
	in addition	
	moreover	

DIRECTNESS: AVOIDING STUPID WRITING

You'd think that being in college would make you a better writer, and that you would gradually improve, from year one to year four (or five, or six). But that's not always the case. At some point, often in their second or third years of college, many students actually become *worse* writers.

How is this possible? Well, they've been reading more academic writing and becoming more at ease with it, and then they start to imitate it. Shouldn't that make them better? Sometimes, yes, but it depends on the quality of what they're reading, and I'm here to tell you that a great deal of academic and professional writing is just plain *bad*. Like this, found in the materials of an actual business:

> Interest in the possible applicability of TRIZ tools and techniques to the world of management and organizational innovation issues continues to grow.

Some of you may be impressed by that—you may think it's sophisticated and complex.

It's not.

It's complicated, that's for sure. But only in the structure of the sentence, not in content. Using that sentence, I'll show you the four key principles for bad writing.

How to write badly in four simple steps

1. Remove any human presence; if that's not possible, at least don't allow anything human to be the subject of the sentence.

2. Turn verbs into nouns (also called nominalizing).

3. Use more words than you need, especially multisyllable words rather than simple ones.

4. Move the verb as far away from the subject as you can.

Let's look more closely to see how our sample sentence observes all four principles:

> Interest in the possible applicability of TRIZ tools and techniques to the world of management and organizational innovation issues continues to grow.

1. **Remove any human presence:** The sentence is "disembodied," which means that it doesn't have a "body," or person. The first word of the sentence is *interest*, so who's interested? Businesses, I assume, so why not say so? Some writers seem

to think that if you remove human beings from sentences, the writing will sound smarter. That may be true—but only to people who don't know better.

2. **Turn verbs into nouns:** *Applicability* is a nominalization of the verb *apply*; *innovation* is a nominalization of *innovate*.

3. **Use more words than you need:** *Possible* and *the world of* are not needed in this sentence.

4. **Move the verb as far away from the subject as you can:** The subject is *interest*, and the verb is *continues*; there are eighteen words between the two, which makes it extremely difficult to connect them. Our most basic desire in English sentences is for a subject and a verb, preferably close together.

The guiding principle of this kind of writing is this: If it's hard to read, you must have to be smart in order to write it.

Good writers know that this principle is wrong; furthermore, following it reveals a contempt for the reader that more people should be aware of. (For example, when political and business leaders communicate with you in this way, you should demand to know why they want to make their policies and practices harder rather than easier to understand. Do they have something to hide?)

Here's how the sentence could be written more clearly, without any loss of meaning:

> Businesses can become more innovative in management and organization when they apply TRIZ tools and techniques.

I'm not absolutely certain I've said what the original writer intended—but that's because his/her writing is unclear. At any rate, I think I'm close. And I've taken a sentence that was twenty-two words and reduced it to fifteen words (32 percent more efficient!); also, it has a real subject (businesses), followed immediately by a verb, and this combination of changes makes the sentence far easier to read.

CHARACTERS AND ACTIONS

If you learn to think of your sentences in terms of characters and actions, you can avoid three of the four principles for bad writing. (The only one that's not covered is #3, about unnecessary words; see previous section of this chapter for more on how to remedy that problem.)

A **character** is what the sentence is really *about*. It usually takes a human form (I, he, she, managers, readers, Canadians, etc.), but it can also be a thing (corn, lamps, a football, etc.). It can be a noun or pronoun.

An **action** is what a character does. It's always a verb.

Putting those two elements—character and action—together at the beginning of the sentence is the simplest way to form a sentence.

With the TRIZ sentence above, my first goal was to figure out who the "characters" were, and my best guess was *businesses*. Once I chose that as the character, I asked myself what I thought businesses were *doing* (action) in the sentence, and I determined that it had something to do with innovation. I wanted to turn that into a verb, but it sounded strange as *Businesses innovate*, so I wrote it as *can become more innovative*, which is fine in this case, I think. The second action, though, is a better example: *Businesses can become more innovative ... when they apply* ....

* * *

English is a flexible, adaptable language, but when writers violate the principles that make it work, they create sentences that don't communicate effectively. The first principle of English grammar is that we want characters to come first, and actions to follow them. Mess with this basic formula too much, and you risk losing your readers or listeners.

I'm simplifying this somewhat, of course. Great writing rarely follows this rule with absolute consistency. Often, other small elements enter into the first parts of a sentence, adding to the compexity and rhythm of the ideas.

FINAL THOUGHTS

Does this scenario sound familiar? You've waited until the day before a paper is due to start working on it. You stay up until three in the morning to finish it, get

---

Note: I am indebted to writer and English professor Joseph M. Williams for some key concepts: characters and actions, and nominalization. Professor Williams' books on style are outstanding, and I recommend them highly; please see *Style: Lessons in Clarity in Grace*, or its more compact version, *Style: The Basics of Clarity and Grace*.

a few hours sleep, finish the works-cited page, give it a title, and print it. You rush to campus, make it to class just in time, and triumphantly hand in your paper.

Then, when you get the paper back, you see that the professor has marked several mistakes you could've found if you'd left yourself more time. And the grade reflects all those careless mistakes. (In my class, a sloppy paper with more than a couple of careless errors will never get a grade above a C.)

Take time to edit and proofread—at least an hour, if not more. Also, the more time you can allow to pass before doing the editing, the better. If you have a little distance from your work, you're more likely to notice problems.

Turning in a polished paper—even one with some flaws in thinking—is almost sure to get you a better grade than one with obvious errors and awkward sentences.

chapter 6

BEYOND CORRECTNESS:
SENTENCE SOPHISTICATION

There's a moral force in a sentence when it comes out right.
It speaks the writer's will to live.

~ Don DeLillo

The best way to develop sophistication in your writing is to read—and imitate—good writing. To do this, pay attention to how professional writers structure their sentences, and how these decisions can extend not only the length of their sentences but also the depth of their thinking.

But you want to increase the sophistication of your writing *now*. First, though, a piece of advice on what *not* to do: don't substitute "thesaurus words" for your simple ones. Of course, the vocabulary you use will play a role in how sophisticated your writing sounds, but it's generally more productive to learn how to write different kinds of sentences. Doing this will force you to think more deeply about what you're saying, and it's in this extension of your thinking that the real sophistication lies. This chapter will cover four ways to do this.

- Participle
- Appositive
- Absolute
- Dash

About the terminology: The first three terms are grammatical, meaning that they refer to the structure of sentences. The last one, the dash, is not a grammatical constuction but a mark of punctuation. (You should also know that many professional writers couldn't explain the difference between an appositive and an absolute, but they use these constructions all the time. In other words, learn the concepts, but don't get hung up on the terminology.)

PARTICIPLE

A participle is a verb form, such as *running, jumped, thought,* or *eaten.* Participles generally end in –ing or –ed (or some other form of the past tense).

1. Take a simple sentence, like this:

> Kevin was the neighborhood bully.

2. Replace the period with a comma, then make the next word a participle—one that tells us something more about him.

> Kevin was the neighborhood bully, **picking fights**....

3. Then add more information—either an adverb or some prepositional phrases, anything that will tell us more about the action in the participle.

> Kevin was the neighborhood bully, **picking** fights with smaller boys and even some of the girls.

> He was an angry boy, **punching** and **kicking** his way through the fifth grade.

You can also reverse the order:

> Kicking and screaming all the way, Kevin was dragged away from the free donuts in the cafeteria.

I made up a new sentence because the previous examples didn't sound right reversed.

Important note: Whenever you start a sentence with a participle, the thing or person "doing" the participle (*kicking, screaming* above) must come immediately after the comma. The only exception to this is that you could put an adjective before Kevin's name, like this:

> Kicking and screaming all the way, the **red-faced** boy was dragged away from the free donuts in the cafeteria.

(Yes, I changed *Kevin* to *boy* because it didn't sound right with his name there.)

Examples from professional writers, with participles in bold:

> They were bound to work as their fathers had worked, **killing** themselves or **preparing** to kill others.
>
> — Scott Russell Sanders, "The Men We Carry in Our Minds"

This one works slightly differently; it uses the -ed form

> Tacked to one of its walls was a memo, **scrawled** with pink highlighter.
>
> — Lauren Collins, "Friend Game," *The New Yorker*

Here's another one:

> In the evenings and on weekends they worked on their own places, **tilling** gardens that were lumpy with clay, **fixing** broken-down cars, **hammering** on houses that were always too drafty, too leaky, too small.
>
> — Scott Russell Sanders, "The Men We Carry in Our Minds"

That's a sophisticated way of using participles. There are other grammatical elements at work, but the key feature is the serial (meaning: as a series, in a row) use of three participles: *tilling, fixing, hammering*.

Imagine that Sanders were a lesser writer, one who could not produce such a fluid, well-crafted sentence; it might read like this:

WITHOUT PARTICIPLES	In the evenings and on weekends they worked on their own places. They **tilled** gardens that were lumpy with clay, they **fixed** broken-down cars, and they **hammered** on houses that were always too drafty, too leaky, too small.

The sentence conveys a number of memorable physical details, but it's in the sentence's rhythms that the reader feels the suffering of these men.

APPOSITIVE

An appositive is part of a sentence—typically made up of nouns and/or adjectives, but *not* verbs—that relates to another part of a sentence. It gives additional information or explains the other part.

1. Take the same sentence that we were using before:

> Kevin was the neighborhood bully.

2. Replace the period with a comma, then add information about "the neighborhood bully"; this information should not include a verb:

> Kevin was the neighborhood bully, **a mean-spirited kid, a pint-sized terrorist with a cackle for a laugh.**

mean-spirited kid = compound adjective + noun
pint-sized terrorist = compound adjective + noun
with a cackle = prepositional phrase
for a laugh = prepositional phrase

Two Types of Appositives

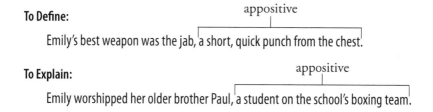

To Define:

appositive

Emily's best weapon was the jab, a short, quick punch from the chest.

To Explain:

appositive

Emily worshipped her older brother Paul, a student on the school's boxing team.

Usually we don't like to separate the subject (*jab*, in the example below) from the verb (*was*), but in this case it might be effective:

> The jab—a short, quick punch from the chest—was Emily's best weapon.

This rearrangement has two potential benefits. First, it allows you to start a sentence with something other than Emily. Second, it places emphasis on the jab. This might be useful if you're focusing more on boxing and less on Emily.

Note: I used dashes in this sentence because I thought commas would look confusing. More on dashes later in this chapter.

Examples from professional writers:

> But toward women I feel something more confused, **a snarl** of shame, envy, wary tenderness, and amazement.

> — Scott Russell Sanders, "The Men We Carry in Our Minds"

> In 1822 Britain passed a law against improper treatment of cattle, **the first animal-welfare legislation** in history.

> — P.J. O'Rourke, "Masters of the Hunt," *Atlantic Monthly*

Creating Appositives in Revision

As you revise your writing, look for sentences that can be combined, particularly when one sentence adds a small amount of information that briefly defines or explains something in the other sentence.

> Emily had known Kevin since preschool. He was once her best friend.

Take the second sentence and turn it into an appositive:

> Emily had known Kevin, once her best friend, since preschool.

It can also be punctuated with dashes (see last part of chapter for more on these), which will give the appositive more emphasis and draw more attention to that information:

> Emily had known Kevin—once her best friend—since preschool.

ABSOLUTE

The absolute is interesting because it is *almost* a complete sentence itself. This is part of what makes it complex and somewhat difficult to use correctly.
An absolute usually begins with a noun or noun phrase, follows with a verb, then includes a prepositional phrase or object. But that's confusing. Read the examples instead of trying to make sense of my explanation.

> Emily stared at Kevin. Her eyes were focused with an animal's ferocious intent.

To turn the second part into an absolute:

> Emily stared at Kevin, her eyes narrowed with an animal's ferocious intent.

You'll notice that the only change is to remove the helping verb *were* from the original. That's what I meant when I said that the absolute is typically very close to a complete thought.

One more example:

> Emily ate dinner in silence. Her thoughts kept drifting back to Kevin.

Revised, using absolutes:

> Emily ate dinner in silence, her thoughts drifting back to Kevin.

That sounds a little strange, so I added one word to get the sense of the word *kept* from the original:

> Emily ate dinner in silence, her thoughts constantly drifting back to Kevin.

An absolute that summarizes:

> Emily had been getting in more fights lately, a trend that disturbed her parents.

The key word that creates the summary is **trend**. The trick here is to find a noun that sums up the idea present in the other part of the sentence.

It's also worth noticing how this type of appositive is more efficient than other, more common constructions. For example, many students would have written the above sentence like this:

AVOID THIS
CONSTRUCTION | Emily had been getting in more fights lately, **which was** a trend that disturbed her parents.

Those two extra words, *which was*, are unnecessary here. The sentence is perfectly acceptable, grammatically—but it's also flabby and graceless.

Combining elements

Here's an example that combines an appositive and a participle:

> Each stag hunt has a "harbourer," a specialist whose job is to watch the herds and select a specific quarry, chosen for its lack of Darwinian promise.

> — P.J. O'Rourke, "Masters of the Hunt," *Atlantic Monthly*

DASH

The dash is a way of separating information. The key difference between the dash and other "separating" marks of punctuation (commas, semi-colons, periods) is that the dash is a stronger interruption, and it generally feels less formal than those other marks.

A word on what a dash is *not*: it's not a hyphen. A hyphen is a punctuation mark that connects two or more words: re-create, ex-wife, door-to-door salesman.

Like other marks of punctuation, the dash has grammatical rules that apply to it. These rules depend on whether you use a single dash or a pair, so we'll discuss these separately.

As a single dash

> Emily walked away from Kevin—and away from fighting too.

In this example, the dash allows you to add another piece of information to the sentence. It could have been done with a comma instead of a dash, but the dash provides more emphasis. It gives the second part of the sentence more weight and importance.

A single dash can also allow the part after the dash to function as a definition (not in a dictionary sense) of what precedes it, like this:

> MySpace, with its cluttered layout, can suggest an online incarnation of the broken-windows theory—surface disorder begetting actual chaos.

> — Lauren Collins, "Friend Game," *The New Yorker*

In that sentence, the end of the sentence explains (or defines, in a sense) broken-windows theory.

TIP: WORD PROCESSING

Creating a dash. . . It seems simple, but word processing programs don't always do what you want them to. So, allow me to explain:

Type two hyphens immediately after Kevin—don't use the space bar.

> Emily walked away from Kevin--

Start typing the next word, again with no spaces after the hyphens. Once you've typed the next word and then hit the space bar, the hyphens will turn into a dash.

> Emily walked away from Kevin—and away

Creating a dash in revision. . . If you want to add a dash to a sentence you've already written, you need to do it a certain way.

Let's say you want to change this comma to a dash.

> Emily walked away from Kevin, and away from fighting too.

Delete the comma and type two hyphens. Make sure there are no spaces before or after the hyphens.

> Emily walked away from Kevin--and away from fighting too.

Move the cursor over to the end of the next word (*and*, in this case) and type a space. The hyphens should turn into a dash, and now you just need to get rid of the extra space after *and*.

> Emily walked away from Kevin—and |away from fighting too.

> Emily walked away from Kevin—and away

There's one other way that a single dash can be used, and it's a bit unusual grammatically.

> He or she, able to play with different personas, is released from some of the petty humiliations of being a middle-schooler—all it takes to be a Ludacris fan is a couple of keystrokes.
>
> – Lauren Collins, "Friend Game," *The New Yorker*

In that sentence, the part that comes after the dash is a complete thought, which means that in this case the dash has the same grammatical "power" as a period or semicolon—it can connect two complete thoughts. (Like the sentence I just wrote.)

A dash always calls some attention to itself, so you should use it sparingly. It's particularly useful when your sentence includes a number of commas; the dash, or paired dashes, can help keep the grammar of your sentence clear.

As a pair of dashes

When you use dashes in a pair, remember that they function almost exactly like parentheses. Grammatically, the principle is identical: Whatever you put inside the dashes can be removed without affecting the grammar of the sentence.

In terms of meaning, too, paired dashes resemble parentheses. What you find inside the dashes is something of an afterthought, an aside, something interesting but not essential to our understanding. What the paired dashes do that parentheses don't is call more attention to the information inside them. Parentheses are like a whispered comment, while dashes are like a poke in the ribs.

> At thirteen, Megan was technically too young to have an account—users are required to be at least fourteen—but MySpace has not instituted any effective means of enforcing its age restrictions.
>
> – Lauren Collins, "Friend Game," *The New Yorker*

The information inside the dashes here is not essential at all—it's simply an extra fact about MySpace that readers may find useful to know.

In the next example, the material inside the dashes has more significance.

> Megan had used a cloth belt—Tina had just bought it for her at Old Navy—to hang herself from a closet organizer.
>
> – Lauren Collins, "Friend Game," *The New Yorker*

The fact that the cloth belt came from Old Navy might seem like a trivial fact, but I would argue that it's not, and that the subtle significance of this detail comes through because of the use of the dashes. The significance is two-fold: First, the belt was purchased by her mother, which reinforces the youth and innocence of Megan; second, the fact that it's from Old Navy conveys a sense of Megan being the "everygirl." It makes her average and ordinary, which connects to larger themes in this essay, namely that the online interactions common among kids this age can have tragic consequences.

That last example shows how sentence construction—and all the small decisions that writers make about how to convey information—is closely tied to the making of meaning.

As many writers have observed, form and content are inseparable.

FINAL THOUGHTS

If you've read and understood most of this chapter, that's great—but it probably won't have much immediate effect on your writing. In order for that to happen, you have to read and pay attention to good writers. Become more analytical in your reading. It doesn't matter if you can say, *Oh, yeah, that's an appositive and an absolute in that sentence*. I confuse them myself. You don't need to become one of those people who can name every grammatical term and principle in the English language. Those people can be annoying—I know, because I used to be one of them.

Good writers tend to have a strong *sense* of language, and this is what you want to try to develop.

My final principle: Good reading leads to good writing leads to good thinking. And vice versa. Each is connected to the other two.

WRITING

READING   THINKING

chapter 7

RESEARCH BASICS

Research means that you don't know,
but are willing to find out.
> ~ Charles Kettering

WHY DO YOU HAVE TO WRITE RESEARCH PAPERS?

The most obvious reason: To get a grade

The problem with this is that it has little to do with you, the writer. What motivation, beyond a grade, do you have for digging deeply into your subject or for caring about making your writing subtle, nuanced, careful? Why would you care? The only person who will read your paper is your professor, and you barely know her.

I raise this question because I want you to find better reasons for writing—reasons that might help you enjoy the writing more and write better papers too.

A less obvious—and better—reason: It makes you smarter

A confession: When I was a college student majoring in philosophy, I never enjoyed writing papers. I loved how reading one essay or book could lead to another; I loved beginning to see the connections among ideas, and how one philosopher's thinking extended or transformed someone's else's work. But I often dreaded the writing. I'd done all the important work of learning about a subject, so why did I have to write about it?

I came to understand, slowly, that it was in the writing that I was really learning how to make sense of what I'd read. Don't get me wrong—I love the idea of reading purely for pleasure. But at the heart of higher education is a different way of interacting with ideas. And that kind of interaction *requires* writing. We need to write in order to really learn *what* we think, and *how* we think it.

In short, our most significant learning takes place when we write. And that's a good reason for writing.

And an even better reason: It improves the world

In Chapter 2, I said that all writing is rhetorical, meaning that at some level it is always trying to persuade the reader to accept the view(s) of the writer.

When this writing enters "the world" (when it is published as an essay or book), it becomes part of what might be called a "larger conversation," and it's in this conversation that writers have the power to improve the world. To use an example that you'll read about later in this chapter: When Michael Pollan wrote his book *The Omnivore's Dilemma*, about how agriculture works in America, he was simply continuing an ongoing conversation about the relationships among farms, industry, business, the environment, the oil industry, and our dining room tables. Plenty of people disagreed with him—but in that disagreement, too, the conversation continued. Pollen doesn't get the last word in the conversation, but he's now part of it, and as a result, people are talking about these issues in new ways. People like me—who never gave much thought to these issues before—are starting to think about where our food comes from and how far it has to travel (and thus, how much oil is used in the process) to get to us.

In a not-so-small way, Pollan has changed the world.

Of course, when you write a paper for a college class, that paper isn't likely to be published and influence how people think about a subject. But if you try to think in those terms, it might help you write more purposeful papers.

EXTENDING THE CONVERSATION

Your reader (that mythical stranger who is interested in your subject matter but doesn't know you—and is not your professor) has two basic expectations about your paper:

1. You have something to say.

This means that your paper is driven by an idea that is at least somewhat new or original. It can't simply say what has been said before—why bother writing it if someone else already has?

2. You are aware of what has already been said.

In order for an intelligent reader to trust you, you must demonstrate that you're familiar with the important work that has been already been done on your subject.

The combination of these two ideas is the basis for "extending the conversation." If you think of any particular subject—global warming, the lives of ancient Romans, the role of bilingual education in language acquisition—you can easily imagine it as a "conversation." Sometimes that conversation becomes angry and unpleasant, but it's still a conversation. Which doesn't mean that it's two-sided, or that it represents only two views. Many conversations have multiple speakers, each with a unique perspective.

Again, I want to stress an important idea that has come up throughout this book: No one ever has the last word. The conversation always continues.

It's easy to see how this way of thinking about writing and research has implications beyond the classroom. Only in a country that preserves real intellectual freedom can ideas be debated so freely. By extension, when your professor asks you to write a paper, he or she is asking you to participate in one of the most important forms of democracy available to us: the ability to think freely and share ideas.

Enough inspiration—let's get to the business.

INTERACTING WITH SOURCE MATERIAL

When you interact with your sources, you're doing two things—first announcing to your reader, "Here's what someone else has to say," and second, in effect, saying, "Here's what I have to say about that."

Writing a paper where you only do the first part—reporting what other people have said/written—is generally pointless. (Some professors do assign papers that are merely reports, though, so make sure you know what your professor expects.)

TIP: FINDING & EVALUATING SOURCES

The easier a source is to find, the less reliable and scholarly it tends to be.

Effort and/or Expertise Needed to Find Source		Quality of Source
Minimal effort No expertise	**Quick Google Search / Wikipedia** You can find a wikipedia entry in a matter of seconds. It will give you some basic (though potentially inaccurate) information, and your professor will think little of it as a source.	Poor
Minimal effort Some expertise	**More Selective Google Search** With slightly more effort, you can find some material on the Internet that's more reliable—articles from a reputable newspaper or magazine (e.g., the *New York Times* or the *Atlantic Monthly*), even some government documents.	Good to Excellent
Some effort Some expertise	**Books** You'll have to leave your computer (briefly), but if you go to the library or use interlibrary loan, you can certainly find books that explore the topic more deeply and from a more academic perspective. Also, if you go to the library, you can consult with research librarians—take advantage of their expertise.	Good to Excellent
Some effort Some expertise	**Academic Journals** If you want to consult the most academically respected sources, you'll need to find peer-reviewed academic journals. Search for these in Google Scholar (see Chapter 8) and the library databases (see Chapter 10)—they're not always easy to find or search, but the effort is worth it.	Generally Excellent

"Here's what someone else has to say."

When you use source material, it's important that you do so responsibly, which means quoting, paraphrasing, or summarizing accurately. Typically, you want to use a *signal phrase* (such as *According to Michael Pollan*) to introduce the source material; this will make it clear that the idea or information belongs to a source, not to you.

Quote: to use the exact words of your source.

Paraphrase: to put someone else's idea into your own words.

Summarize: to state the main idea of a text (or part of a text) in a shortened form.

> **Note:** Usually a summary is only a fraction of the length of the original; you can summarize a three-page essay in a few sentences, but you can't summarize it in three pages—the summary must be a small fraction of the total. For a longer work, like a 300-page novel, you can summarize it in a few sentences or a few paragraphs, depending on how much detail you go into.

"Here's what I have to say about that."

This is where you enter the conversation, and essentially you have three options, with some overlap: to use the source in support of something you're saying, to disagree with the source (and offer a different way of looking at something), or to extend or build upon an idea the source offers. It should always be clear to your reader *why* you're using source material—it should always be in service of something you're developing in your paper.

How much should you quote, paraphrase, or summarize?

The answer to this question depends on a number of factors—the discipline (psychology, linguistics, art history, biology, etc.) you're working in, the type of paper you're writing, and your professor's expectations.

So it's impossible to give you a precise answer. Still, I'm going to suggest that you think about a basic question of proportion. By proportion, I mean this: How much do you quote or paraphrase sources compared to the overall length of your paper?

Let's pretend that you quote or paraphrase five sources for a total of roughly twenty sentences. If you add up all those sentences, how many pages would it amount to? Let's say it adds up to two pages.

Now, how long is your paper? For the sake of this example, let's say it's 10 pages. (I'm sorry—I know this isn't math class, but you'll see how it's useful in a moment.) In other words, the paper is 20 percent source material, 80 percent yours. That's probably fine—for most disciplines, most papers, most professors.

Now imagine that you have those same two pages of source material, but that you're entire paper is only *four* pages long. The math changes significantly: Now the paper is 50 percent source material, 50 percent yours.

That means that we're only reading *you* for half the paper. For most professors, that's probably not enough.

I can't tell you exactly what the percentage should be, but I can make three suggestions:

- Be aware how much of your paper is made up of source material.
- If your paper is more than half source material, that's often too much.
- Talk to your professor about his expectations. From my example, you should be able to examine your paper, make a relatively accurate guess about the proportions and then say to your professor, "I think my paper is about 25 percent source material; does that sound like too much?"

Primary vs. Secondary sources

Many professors will require that you do both primary (meaning first or original) and secondary research. In the excerpt you're about to read, from Michael Pollan's book, his research on prices of particular items at a grocery store is *primary* research. Most likely, he took notes in a grocery store and/or examined advertising from stores. He didn't rely on some other researcher for this information—he examined the "data" himself. If, however, you used Pollan's book as a source, then his book and everything in it would be a *secondary* source.

Primary sources are often pure data (a government census, enrollment figures at a college, city tax records), but they can also be documents created or recorded by "participants" in an event: letters from Civil War soldiers, video of the Kennedy assasination, etc.

Seconday sources, on the other hand, are those that interpret, comment on, analyze or make arguments about those events: a book that argues how Confederate soldiers became increasingly hopeless as the war progressed, an essay proposing a new theory about Kennedy's death, and so on.

SUMMARIZING, PARAPHRASING, AND QUOTING

These three skills are essential in research writing. I'll cover each one separately, and to illustrate I'll use an excerpt from Michael Pollan's book about food and agriculture in America, *The Omnivore's Dilemma*. The following excerpt appears on page 136, in a chapter that discusses how organic food has become a big industry. With all three techniques, it's important to provide the proper citation (for more on this, see Chapter 11 on MLA Documentation).

This excerpt explains how things work in traditional supermarkets.

> Wordy labels, point-of-purchase brochures, and certification schemes are supposed to make an obscure and complicated food chain more legible to the consumer. In the industrial food economy, virtually the only information that travels along the food chain linking producer and consumer is price. Just look at the typical newspaper ad for a supermarket. The sole quality on display here is actually a quantity: tomatoes $0.69 a pound; ground chuck $1.09 a pound; eggs $0.99 a dozen—special this week. Is there any other category of product sold on such a reductive basis? The bare-bones information travels in both directions, of course, and farmers who get the message that consumers care only about price will themselves care only about yield. This is how a cheap food economy reinforces itself.

SUMMARIZING

This is a lot like paraphrasing, with one important difference: When you paraphrase, what you write is roughly equal in length to your source. When you summarize, on the other hand, you're making the original shorter, sometimes much shorter.

The goal of summarizing is to capture the main idea of the source material—whether it's a paragraph, a chapter or an entire book—as accurately as possible. It's an important skill to have as both a reader and a writer, and it's also a great intellectual exercise. (By the way, reading a summary of a book is no substitute for reading the actual book.)

The sentence I wrote immediately before Pollan's paragraph was an informal summary. I've written a new one here that is more precise:

signal phrase

Pollan asserts that the industrial food economy continues to dominate because neither farmers nor traditional grocery stores are motivated to provide any information beyond price to consumers.

You might find it reassuring to know that it took me—the supposed expert in these matters—about five minutes to write that one sentence. I had to keep thinking about which information to include and how the ideas related to each other. I wrote it three different ways before I was satisfied with it.

PARAPHRASING

To paraphrase is to put a writer's idea in your own words. Most students go about this in the most counter-productive way: they stare at the original sentence and try to think of synonyms for the key words, then put together a "new" sentence that has different words but often sounds awkward.

THE IMPORTANCE OF SIGNAL PHRASES

In a typical research paper, you might use four or five (or many more) sources. Every time you move from one source to another, it's a moment of potential confusion for the reader, particularly when you're also making your own assertions. When you use signal phrases consistently, it helps the reader keep track of who's saying what.

Instead, the best way to paraphrase is this:

1. Read the sentence(s) closely and be sure that you understand everything the writer is saying. Pay particular attention to how ideas relate to each other, especially when the writer is showing causality (one thing causing another).

2. Close the book, or the Web page, or whatever it is you're reading.

3. Reconstruct the idea in your head in language that makes sense to you. If you're not looking at the original, you'll be less inclined to repeat its wording or structure, and the sentence you write will sound more natural.

4. Start writing, still without looking at the original. Don't worry if you repeat a word or two that appeared in the original.

5. Compare your version to the original. The idea from the original should be intact, but the new sentence should sound like *your* writing. Now, if necessary, think of synonyms to replace key words you repeat from the original.

Here's an example where I paraphrase one of Pollan's sentences. His sentence:

> The bare-bones information travels in both directions, of course, and farmers who get the message that consumers care only about price will themselves care only about yield.

First, I made sure I understood the idea—that farmers have changed their practices *because* (causality) they know what motivates consumers.

This is what I came up with. (It might not be the finest paraphrase you'll ever read, but it does the job. The ideas are intact, as is the relationship between them, the cause and effect. And I believe that the voice is mine, not Pollan's.)

signal phrase

Pollan asserts that because many farmers believe consumers are only concerned with cost, the farmers then focus only on how much of any particular crop they can produce (136).

Here's another version, without a signal phrase:

Farmers who know that consumers are concerned only with cost will in turn focus only on how much of any particular crop they can produce (Pollan 136).

I can't emphasize the importance of the citation enough. Even if you paraphrase, you still must give credit to your sources for their ideas. If you don't, it's plagiarism.

QUOTING

Once you've decided to quote rather than paraphrase, you have one more decision to make: Do you want to quote an entire sentence (or more), or do you want to quote only part of a sentence?

HOW DO YOU DECIDE WHETHER TO QUOTE OR PARAPHRASE?

Your first instinct should be to paraphrase. It's generally better to use your own language—and it's good intellectual practice to put someone else's ideas into your own words.

I'm not saying that you shouldn't quote your sources; quotations are essential, and they can help you be more efficient and accurate. The danger is that when you quote too much, your paper may sound more like a jumble of other writers than *you*.

You need a good reason to quote a source rather than paraphrase it; here are three:

1. Your source says something in a particularly compelling or interesting way. If the specific language the source uses is important to our understanding of the idea, you should quote that language.
2. Your source says something that is similar to, or supportive of, a point you're making. In this case, the exact words of the source can help back up a claim you're making.
3. Your source says something that you disagree with, and part of your analysis focuses on shades of meaning that can be seen in the precise word choice.

Quoting an entire sentence

This is the easiest way to quote because there are no complicated rules about punctuation.

I'll choose a sentence that fits my first reason for quoting—the one that says to quote a writer when he or she says something in a particularly interesting way.

Here's what the sentence would look like in my essay:

signal phrase

Michael Pollan wonders, "Is there any other category of product sold on such a reductive basis?" (136).

That one is a little unusual because it includes a question mark, so I'll quote another sentence to show a more common example:

> As Michael Pollan observes, "The bare-bones information travels in both directions, of course, and farmers who get the message that consumers care only about price will themselves care only about yield" (136).

It looks simple, but many students make mistakes with this kind of quotation. It's essential that you have some kind of introduction for the quotation. You should never have a sentence that's only a quotation without any kind of context. (The "context" I've provided above, *As Michael Pollan observes*, is minimal; sometimes you'll want to do more, but generally this is adequate.)

Quoting part of a sentence

This is more common than quoting an entire sentence. It allows you to partially paraphrase a writer's idea but still show his or her exact wording, briefly. Quoting part of a sentence is useful when a writer says something memorable or interesting—or simply difficult to paraphrase—in just a word or phrase. Here I quote part of Pollan's first sentence:

signal phrase

> Pollan claims that stores like Whole Foods use these techniques to "make an obscure and complicated food chain more legible to the consumer" (136).

The key to making the partial quotation work is to write your sentence so that the quoted material flows grammatically within the entire sentence. In other words, if you took the quotation marks away, the sentence would still make sense grammatically—it would still sound like a good sentence. (Though, of course, you wouldn't want to actually do this because that would be plagiarism.)

You can also quote a single word, which puts great emphasis on that word:

> Pollan describes the contemporary agricultural economy as "industrial" (136).

When I was writing that sentence, I had the feeling that I wanted to disagree with Pollan—something about calling attention to that single word *industrial* made me think that the next sentence should question that word choice.

Of course, I could also have emphasized that word because I wanted to assert that Pollan's description is accurate and even revealing.

signal phrase

Pollan describes the contemporary agricultural process as "industrial" (136); this makes plain the connections between farming and big business and reveals their shared qualities: both are dirty, dangerous, and almost always polluted.

Reminder: This is just a quick overview of the key things you need to know about quoting. In Chapter 11, I cover additional guidelines that you're likely to need: how to use ellipses (the three dots) and brackets (for words that you change in a quotation), and how to quote someone who's being quoted.

USEFUL VERBS

all are better than *says / states*

asserts	observes
claims	maintains
argues	suggests

PLAGIARISM

Each semester I catch a student or two or three who plagiarize. These students get zeros on their papers, and most tend to fail the course. To rework Nike's old slogan: Just don't do it.

WHAT IT IS

Plagiarism can take many forms, and some are worse than others. Most simply it means taking something that is not yours (an idea, a statistic, a piece of research, or an entire paper) and presenting it as your own. This is intellectual theft, and it violates everything that colleges and universities value.

HOW TO AVOID IT

To begin with, try to find a topic for your research that you care about; I realize that this is sometimes difficult, since many professors place limitations on your topics. If you can't choose your own topic, try to find some aspect of the topic that is meaningful to you. When you care about your subject, you're more likely to want to do your own thinking about it.

PLAGIARISM AND RESEARCH

As you research, try to be organized as you work with your sources. Highlight passages that you plan on quoting, paraphrasing, or summarizing. Develop a number or symbol system to help you keep track of sources. I've seen far too many students suffer because they put off doing their in-text citations until they're finished writing their papers; this is a terrible idea because at that stage you then have to look up all the page numbers again. Maintain a system as you take notes and as you write. When in doubt, give credit to a source. If you're not sure whether or not you need an in-text citation, provide one.

Don't put the paper off until the last minute. A research paper requires careful attention to detail; it's generally not the kind of thing you can pull off the night before it's due. And it's definitely in your best interest to have all of your citations (in-text and works cited) done in your first draft. That way your professor can let you know if there are problems.

MY IDEALISM

I am an idealist: I believe that if you're in college, you should care about matters of the mind. You should be intellectually curious, willing to engage new ideas and think deeply about them. You should also be willing (and happy, really) to do the serious research that higher education requires. If you're not—and if you're thinking about "borrowing" a paper instead of writing one yourself—you should seriously reconsider whether or not you belong in college at all.

chapter 8

INTERNET RESEARCH

*Getting information off the Internet is like taking a drink
from a fire hydrant.*
> ~ Mitch Kapor

Everyone knows how to search the Internet, but this chapter is meant to help you search more productively and efficiently—and also to evaluate your results.

Let's say that you're writing a paper that responds to some issue in Michael Pollan's book *The Omnivore's Dilemma* (see previous chapter for excerpt). For the sake of this example, I'll assume that you've narrowed your topic somewhat and decided to address what Pollan calls the "industrial food economy." Of course, the specific focus of your paper will determine how you search, but let's start with some basic principles.

A BASIC GOOGLE SEARCH

There are a variety of ways to do this, but I'm going to lead you through a couple of basic searches using Google (google.com), since that search engine is most likely already familiar to you.

The most obvious thing to do is to search for *industrial food economy*, right? Sure, why not…

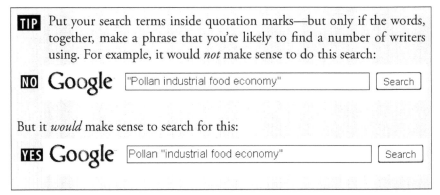

In this case, though, for the sake of simplicity and because we want to find things that don't necessarily make reference to Pollan, we'll leave out his name. In the search below, we'll only get results that include the exact phrase *industrial food economy*.

EVALUATING THE RESULTS

This is where things become more complicated, and the best piece of advice I can give you about which sites to consider for your paper is to use both common sense and critical thinking. Let's look at the first result, from TreeHugger.com.

Hamilton Farmers Market. Credit: Communications Branch of the Ontario Ministry of Agriculture and Food

The title is "Creative Food Economy Emerges in Ontario," which makes me think that this probably isn't a great source for a paper, mainly because the focus on Ontario (part of Canada) makes the subject matter too narrow. Also, at the bottom of the page, I can see who publishes the site:

© TreeHugger.com 2010 | Visitor Agreement | Privacy Policy | Discovery Communications, LLC

Discovery Sites: Discovery Channel | TLC | Animal Planet | Discovery Health | Science Channel | Discovery Store Planet Green | HowStuffWorks | Discovery Times | Discovery Kids | HD Theater | FitTV | Petfinder | Turbo

The "publisher" is TreeHugger.com, which means nothing to me. But when I continue reading, I find that the site is clearly connected to the Discovery Channel, which means that it's more about entertainment (and profit) than education or serious research. Hey, I'm not picking on Discovery Channel—I watch it myself and find it interesting and informative. But I wouldn't rely on it as a source if I were writing a research paper.

Two sites, compared

Here are the third and fourth results from the search:

Bringing the Food Economy Home « OrganicFoodee.com - Jan 9
Bringing the Food Economy Home provides an eye-opening analysis of the problems caused by the globalised **industrial food economy**. As the writers point out, ...
www.organicfoodee.com/books/foodeconomy/ - Cached -

Reclaiming Food Sovereignty from the Global Economy - Jan 9
We have created an industrial economy, including an **industrial food economy**, which is inevitably trending toward entropy. It is simply not sustainable. ...
web.missouri.edu/~ikerdj/papers/Hartwick-Food.htm - Cached -

"Bringing the Food Economy Home" sounds like a reasonably serious title for a page, but the name of the site, OrganicFoodee.com, does not inspire confidence. It sounds informal and casual, not academic or scholarly. The fourth result, on the other hand, "Reclaiming Food Sovereignty from the Global Economy," sounds more academic. Also notice that the URL is web.missouri.edu, the web site of a large research university. Not every site that ends in .edu will bring you to reliable information, but it often does.

Let's look at both pages more closely to determine if either of them would be useful as a source for a college paper.

Now you know a lot more. The fact that the site calls itself "your organic lifestyle magazine" should confirm what I suggested earlier—namely, that it wouldn't be a very reliable source of information. This is not to say that you couldn't learn from the site, or even get ideas for your paper. But it's not the kind of source you want for most college papers. (An exception to this judgment: If you're writing about how popular concern for organic food has grown, then you might find it useful to examine the popularity and profitability of sites like this.)

You should also notice that what appears on this page is actually a review of a book, and maybe the book would be worth reading for your research. In short, even pages that don't look useful can contain something worth exploring. But do so cautiously, and always with an awareness of the quality of sources you intend to use in your paper. Your reader wouldn't take your paper seriously if all of your sources were like OrganicFoodee.com.

Now let's look at the fourth result more closely.

Reclaiming Our Food Sovereignty from the Global Economy[i]

John Ikerd[ii]

Most Americans probably don't give much thought to the security of their food systems. They may have heard or read something about our food systems being an easy target for terrorists. However, most probably believe, with some justification, that such an attack would have no more effect on them personally than did the terrorist attack on the World Trade Center. A disruption of our food systems might create a scarcity of some products, higher food prices for a while, or some other temporary inconvenience. But Americans in general can depend on having an adequate quantity and variety of safe and healthful foods, readily accessible at a reasonable cost – so we are led to believe. Food security may be a concern for people of less developed, weaker nations, or maybe even for developed nations that lack an ability to produce food. But, we have the most productive economy, the most powerful military, and the most productive agriculture in the world; surely, our food systems are secure.

This is just the first paragraph of a long document. Is it a source you could use? How do you decide? There are two key questions that will help you determine how reliable it is as a potential source: Who publishes the site, and who wrote the material you're reading?

Who publishes the site?

We already know that this site is from the University of Missouri. If you go to the bottom of the page, there's no publisher listed—but there is other information that may be helpful.

---

[i] Presented at Hartwick College guest lecture series, Food in Our Lives, Oneonta, NY, November 3, 2005.

[ii] John Ikerd is Professor Emeritus, University of Missouri, Columbia, MO – USA; author of, *Sustainable Capitalism: A Matter of Common Sense,* http://kpbooks.com; website: http://www.ssu.missouri.edu/faculty/jikerd.

[iii] For a complete discussion of differences in industrial and sustainable systems, see John Ikerd, *Sustainable Capitalism: A Matter of Common Sense,* 2005, Kumarian Press, Inc., Bloomfield, CT, available through <http://kpbooks.com>.

The first note tells me that the paper was presented as a lecture at a college, which makes it seem relatively trustworthy.

Who wrote what you're reading?

If you look at the second note, above, you see that the author is a professor and that he has written a book on a related topic. These are both good signs. Again, it doesn't mean that what this paper says is *true*, but it does mean that it's a reasonable source to use in a college paper.

If you're not sure what kind of qualifications the author has, do a Google search and see if you can find out who he works for and where he's been published. If the sources are all blogs, for example, you should probably rule him out as a serious source. If, however, he's had his work published in reputable newspapers and magazines, he could be a good general commentator on your topic. If he's a working scholar who publishes articles in academic journals, then he's definitely a good source.

Wikipedia?

Factory farming - Wikipedia, the free encyclopedia
The issues include the efficiency of **food** production; animal welfare; whether it is .....
Industrial production of pigs and poultry is an important source of GHG ... This tells us that
dairy farms are good for Pennsylvania's **economy**. ...
en.wikipedia.org/wiki/Factory_farming - Cached - Similar - 🗩 ⊼ ☒

No matter what you search for, it seems, Wikipedia is likely to have an entry. In general, you should use Wikipedia only for background information, and you should verify anything you read there with other sources. (You did know that *anyone* can write or edit almost all Wikipedia entries, right? The obvious result of this very democratic approach is that errors—some created by people to amuse themselves, others because they have some kind of agenda—are common.) Most professors do not want to see Wikipedia as a source in your papers.

INTERNET SEARCHES BY AUTHOR AND TITLE

If you've narrowed your paper topic somewhat, you should have some decent search terms already. If you don't, though, here are two suggestions for other ways to search:

Author name: Do a search for the author of anything you've read on your topic. Often, the author has written other works that may explore similar or related subject matter. You'll also find other writers commenting on that author's work.

Work title: This is the same principle as searching for an author's name. If it's a book, you're certain to find book reviews (below), which can be useful.

The problem with book reviews is that they usually focus on whether or not the book is good; reviewers don't typically express opinions about the subject matter of the book itself. A review of Pollan's book, for example, might question how Pollan organized the book, or his style of writing. But it probably wouldn't question the ideas and suggest different conclusions Pollan could have come to. So, if you're writing a paper where you're exploring different views on a subject, you'd be better off with other types of sources, like a commentary piece where a writer is objecting to Pollan's ideas. This one, below, is from *Slate* (slate.com), one of my favorite sites for commentary on current issues.

An economist's critique of **The Omnivore's Dilemma**. - By Tyler ...
Nov 1, 2006 ... In **The Omnivore's Dilemma**: A Natural History of Four Meals, food writer and UC-Berkeley professor Michael Pollan examines three American ...
www.**slate**.com/id/2152675/ - Cached - Similar

SEARCHING BEYOND GOOGLE

Okay, not exactly *beyond* Google, but beyond the ways most of us ordinarily use Google. This section will introduce you to Google Scholar and Google Books, two great resources that are extremely easy to use.

GOOGLE SCHOLAR—on basic Google screen, click on **more**, scroll down to **Scholar**.

These results that you see on the next page are quite different from the previous searches, mainly in that they're all scholarly articles. These aren't necessarily the only kinds of sources you need in college papers, but they are ones you should learn how to find and use more routinely. Quoting from an article in *Time* magazine is fine up to a point, but when you quote from scholarly sources, your reader will take you more seriously.

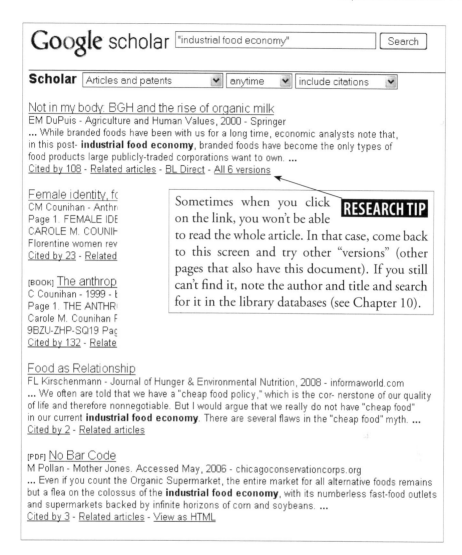

Let's look at the fourth result, "Food as Relationship."

Unlike a regular Web page, a typical result from a Google Scholar search will take you straight to the article, but sometimes you'll only get an abstract (see below), as is the case here.

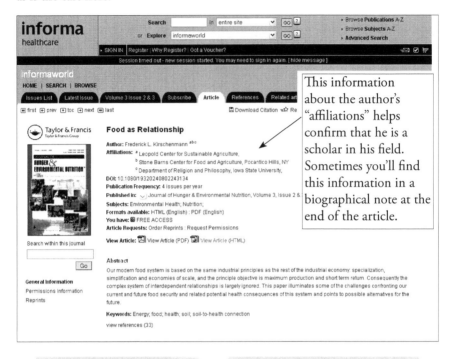

This information about the author's "affiliations" helps confirm that he is a scholar in his field. Sometimes you'll find this information in a biographical note at the end of the article.

WHAT'S A PDF?

PDF stands for "portable document format," and it means that you're seeing a picture of the original document. One advantage of a PDF is that it's easier to document. See Chapter 11.

WHAT'S AN ABSTRACT?

An abstract is a brief summary of an academic article. It's useful because it tells you, quickly, what the article is about as well as the basic argument the author is trying to make. In the sciences, abstracts also tell you how the author conducted the research.

Reading the abstract should help you decide if you want to read more of this article. If you do, you have a couple of options.

In this case, the site will allow you to look at a PDF of the article, or an HTML (Web) page. Given the choice, always opt for the PDF.

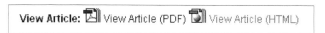

Here's what the PDF looks like. You can enlarge each page for easier reading or print it. Also note the find box; see instructions on next page for how to use it.

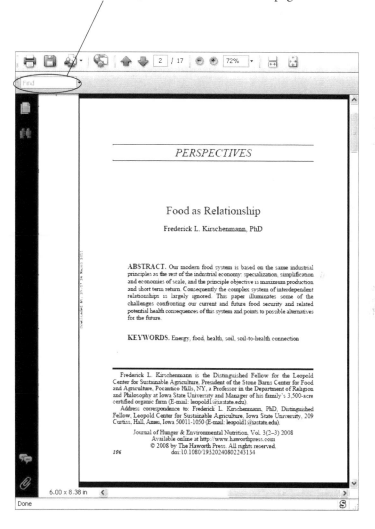

If you're in a hurry (or just a little lazy) . . .

Let's say you just want to find where the author of the article we were just looking at talks about industrialization of food. (This is particularly useful when you find articles that only slightly apply to your area of research.)

Use the **Find** function. On normal Web pages—or any other document—use CTRL + F. In a PDF document, **Find** is at the top of the screen:

In this case, I just put in the word *industrial*. Below you can see one of the places where that word appears. If I hit the ENTER button on the keyboard, it takes me to the next appearance of the word, highlighted in blue.

Frederick L. Kirschenmann   *109*

FOOD IN THE INDUSTRIAL ECONOMY

The soil/food/health connection is not the only relationship we ignore in our modern food system. In fact, our modern industrial culture tends to view not only food but almost all of reality as a collection of fragments (things) rather than a web of relationships. Modern philosophers trace this tendency to the 17th-century scientific revolution. Rene Descartes wanted science to become a "universal mathematics," which, of course, tended to reduce all of reality to measurable things and ignored dynamic relationships. It should not be surprising, therefore, that we have reduced our understanding of healthy food to an ingredient list.

GOOGLE BOOKS

This resource seems to be growing every day. You won't find the full text of many books, but you can read large excerpts from quite a few, which makes it a great way to preview books before you decide what you want to get at your library. Click on **more.**

Click on **Books**.

And here are some of the results, using the same search terms as before.

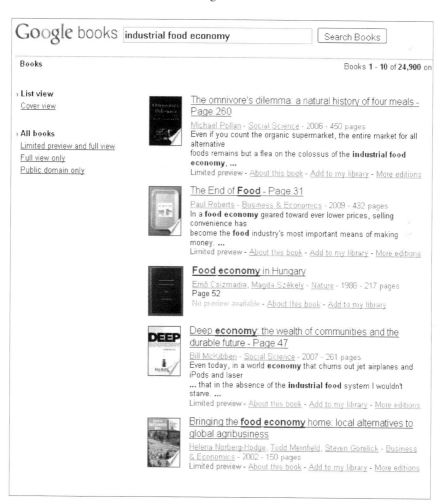

Not surprisingly, Michael Pollan's book appears first, as he uses the phrase "industrial food economy" a number of times. (I chose not to include the quotation marks in this example because I got better results—I tried it both ways.)

I found the last book potentially interesting, and it immediately struck me as familiar. Then I remembered that this was the book being reviewed at OnlineFoodee.com. Based on the title and subtitle (*Local Alternatives to Global Agribusiness*), I think it could be an excellent source. I might check to see who the authors are, and make sure that it's published by a legitimate company. Being "published" doesn't necessarily make a book reliable, but some publishers are better than others.

I won't be able to read all of this book on Google Bookse, but I can certainly see enough of it, including the Table of Contents, to know if I want to try to find it at a local library.

I first click on **Contents** at the top of the page. Here I can see all of the chapter titles.

I choose Chapter 6—and here it is.

6

Food and Community

[There] isn't much community inside a big supermarket. There, we shop as isolated individuals, each in our own private world. Gone are the relationships with the soil, the grower, and, for the most part, even the distributor. Do you know the name of the produce manager in your supermarket? Or anything about his or her family?

—Art Gish, *Food We Can Live With*

IN ECONOMIES WHERE THE GAP between the richest and poorest is relatively narrow and no one lacks the necessities of life, anger and frustration are minimized, while feelings of mutual interdependence—the essence of community—are strong. Such circumstances are common in prosperous local economies, which tend to spread their gains evenly through the entire community. This is not the direction economic globalization is taking us: it is instead leading to an ever-widening gap between rich and poor, enabling some to accumulate vast fortunes while relegating others to abject poverty. In 1960, the income of the richest fifth of the global population was thirty times that of the poorest fifth; by 1997 the gap more than doubled, with the richest fifth receiving seventy-four times more than the poorest fifth.[1]

However, when I try to read a few pages into this chapter, I find missing pages:

> Pages 53-77 are not part of this book preview
>
> **78   Bringing the Food Economy Home**

This is pretty common with books on Google. Still, there's a lot of this book that I *can* read, certainly enough to decide if I want to check it out from the library (see Chapter 9: Library Research).

One more tip

Works-cited entries are a great resource for researchers. Many books—not just scholarly ones—will include a list of sources the author used. Michael Pollan's book has an extensive list of sources; these are some he used in Chapter 2:

> In writing about the rise of industrial agriculture I also drew on the following works:
>
> Kimbrell, Andrew. *The Fatal Harvest Reader: The Tragedy of Industrial Agriculture* (Washington, D.C.: Island Press, 2002).
>
> Manning, Richard. *Against the Grain* (New York: North Point Press, 2004).
>
> Morgan, Dan. *Merchants of Grain* (New York: Viking, 1979).
>
> Russell, Edmund. *War and Nature: Fighting Humans and Insects with Chemicals from World War I to Silent Spring* (Cambridge, U.K.: Cambridge University Press, 2001).
>
> Schwab, Jim. *Raising Less Corn and More Hell: Midwestern Farmers Speak Out* (Urbana: University of Illinois Press, 1988). See the interview with George Naylor beginning on page 111.

A "HYBRID" SEARCH

The great strength of the Internet is in linking—the easy movement from one page to the next, where one idea or subject offers an immediate connection to related ideas. To take advantage of this as a researcher, you might want to try what I call a "hybrid" approach, one that combines Google Books and Amazon. com (or another large online bookseller; Amazon has been most useful for me because it's the largest). Start by finding any book related to your topic on Amazon (or wherever). I chose one from the Google Books search.

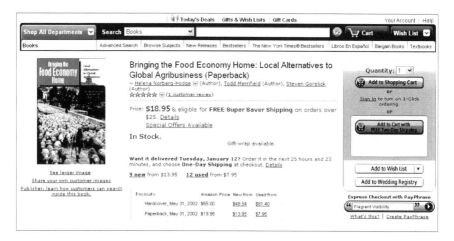

Just a short scroll down the screen you'll find other, similar books. These (and those on the next screen) were bought by customers who looked at *Bringing the Food Economy Home*.

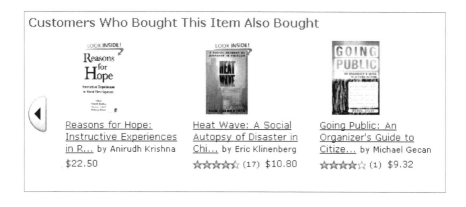

You can also find "tags" (created by customers); clicking on these will lead you to books that have been tagged with specific words, like *sustainable*.

The second book, *Recipe for America*, looks promising.

The *Look Inside* feature allows you to see the table of contents. But first, you should try to determine whether or not this is a quality source. It gets a high rating from Amazon readers, but you can also see what a professional thinks of it by scrolling down to *Editorial Reviews*.

A few pages back, I said that reviews weren't always a great source for your paper; I stand by that. In this case, though, I'm suggesting that you use the professional (rather than reader) reviews to help you decide if the book is appropriate for a college research paper.

This review comes from *Publisher's Weekly*, a respected magazine in the publishing world. From this, you can learn a couple of important things about the book. First, it seems to be a more personal—and not scholarly—book, which limits its usefulness somewhat. Second, this reviewer is not impressed by the author's skill in constructing an argument. So it might not be a great source for information. But if you're interested in writing about how the "local food" movement has flaws that largely go unquestioned, this book might be useful.

Editorial Reviews

From Publishers Weekly

The evils of industrial agriculture are rehashed in this impassioned but sketchy exposé. Food activist and blogger Richardson ticks off a familiar menu of food-system dysfunctions: overreliance on pesticides and fertilizer, exploited farmers and workers, horribly abused livestock, obese children who are fed subsidized junk food in school. (She personalizes her critique with reportage from a stint working at Whole Foods and recollections of a period in her life when a lack of access to fresh produce led her to gain weight on a diet of ice cream and beer.) She contrasts these ills with a vision of sustainable agriculture long on bucolic impressionism—the baby lambs head-butted their mothers enthusiastically and wagged their tails—and short on systematic analysis. The author's rabid advocacy of locavorism is especially myopic; she brushes past the costliness and impracticality—When buying eggs I ask the farmer how many chickens they own and if these chickens are on pasture—and ignores critics who argue that locavorism is an energy-inefficient fad. Only the choir will be convinced by Richardson's shallow take on these complex issues.

FINAL THOUGHTS

Six or seven years ago, I didn't allow my students to use "Internet souces" in their papers because at the time, it was hard to find reliable, quality research materials online. Things have changed dramatically. The Internet has become an incredibly powerful tool for research, so much so that maybe you wonder why we even need libraries anymore. . . . (But we do; keep reading.)

chapter 9

LIBRARY RESEARCH

*I find that a great part of the information I have
was acquired by looking something up and finding
something else on the way.*
                                    ~ Franklin P. Adams

Who needs libraries when we have the Internet?

Libraries in America are changing. Not long ago they were stuffy places where
school-marmish librarians kept busy shushing unruly children. Now, you'll find
computers, video games, DVDs, CDs and art galleries, and no one's shushing
anyone. Some libraries—particularly on college campuses—now have coffee bars
and overstuffed chairs, so that they look and feel more like a Barnes & Noble
than an old-fashioned library.

But one of the best reasons to go the libary isn't for *what* you'll find there, but
who—namely, reference librarians. They love helping people find information,
and they tend to be very, very good at it. So take advantage of their knowledge
and resourcefulness. (You still don't necessarily need to physically go to the library
because many colleges also offer live online chatting with reference librarians.)

Searching the library catalog has become a lot more like a Google search—
simpler and more intuitive. You still have to be careful with your search terms,
but you can move from one source to another, related one much more easily
now. And you don't have to read any advertising or worry about clicking on
something that's going to put a virus on your computer. In short, the library is
relevant again.

A BASIC SEARCH

Building on the previous chapter, let's start with the simple search for a specific author. Go to your college's home page and click on **Library**.

Important Note for HCC Students: The search directions over the next few pages will likely be changing early in 2012. Ask your professor for an up-to-date handout, or write to me (fcooksey@hcc.edu) to request one via email.

At many libraries, you'll need to select the library catalog; on this page, however, there's a search field here.

For the sake of this example, let's assume that you want to find a book by an author you're already familiar with, like Michael Pollan.

Start by using the pull-down menu to change the search field from **Keyword** to **Author**.

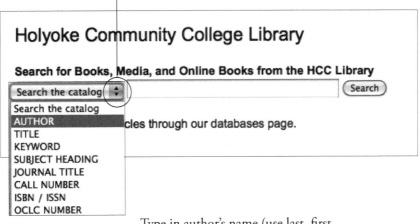

Type in author's name (use last, first name if last name is common).

Here are the first four of nine books. If you want the third book, note that it says *Check Shelves*. You should be able to find that book and check it out now.

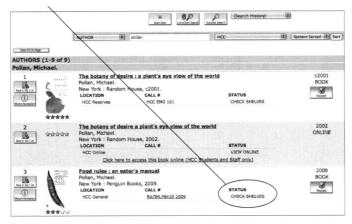

Write down the call number and go find it.

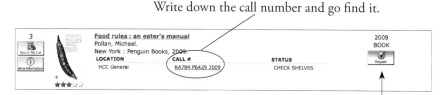

If the book is checked out, you have a couple of options. The easiest is to request it from another library. In this case, the button is called *Request*, but in most cases it will say *Place Hold*.

A MORE COMPLEX SEARCH

Let's say you want to find that book, *Bringing the Food Economy Home: Local Alternatives to Global Agribusiness,* by Helena Norberg-Hodge.

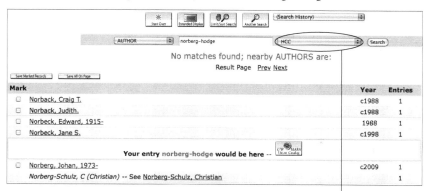

It appears that HCC doesn't have any books by this author. (I checked to make sure I spelled her name correctly.) But right now the system is only searching HCC.

The next step is to change this to some other library; for most students, the better option is to have the system search all the libraries in your region. In this case, use the pull-down menu to select *All Western MA Libraries.*

The search returned six results; here's the book I was looking for:

You can see which libraries have the book; if one of those is convenient for you, simply go there and pick it up. Otherwise, request that it be sent to you.

Two terms: "the stacks" and "holds"

If the book is available in your library, the call number might indicate that it's in "the stacks." These are the rows and rows (and often, floors and floors) of books on shelves. Be aware that larger colleges may have more than one library—make sure you know which building to search in.

Often, with a new and/or popular book, other people have placed "holds" on the book and are waiting for it. You can place a hold on the book too, but be aware that it could take weeks or months before you actually get it. For most books, though, it typically only takes a few days.

A KEYWORD SEARCH

Keyword searches in library catalogs have improved a great deal over the last few years, but they're still not quite like a Google search.

TIP Use fewer words than you would in a Google search, and limit them to *key* words. In Google, the search for *industrial food economy* got 120 million results. Here it gets four. Not four million. Four. One-two-three-four. Think about it.

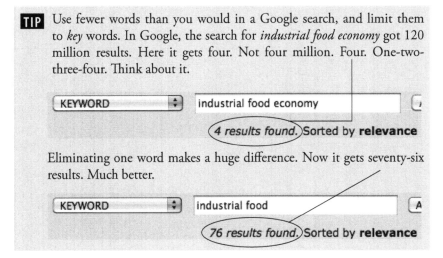

Eliminating one word makes a huge difference. Now it gets seventy-six results. Much better.

Note how the results are organized—*Highly relevant title entries* first, then *Very relevant*, etc.

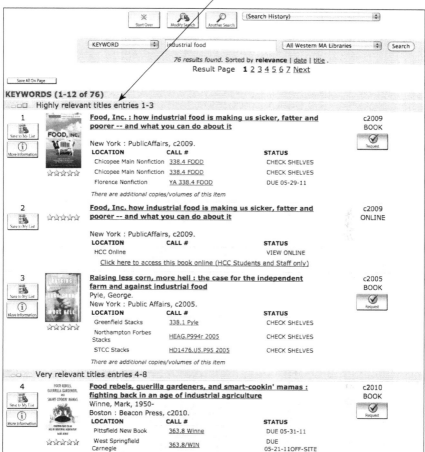

Browse the titles to find a book that interests you. You might also look at the date of publication (generally, the more recent the better) to help make a decision. Notice also that the first book, *Food, Inc.*, can be accessed online. The online version of the book looks better than most books in Google Books (the page is cleaner looking), and it has a number of search tools, making it a good tool for research.

Once you find one good book on your subject, it's easy to find related books. On the next page, I'll suggest a couple of ways to do that: *Tags*, and *Similar Books*.

When you click on one of the books, you'll see many similarities to the pages of commercial booksellers (Amazon, etc.). One is *Tags*.

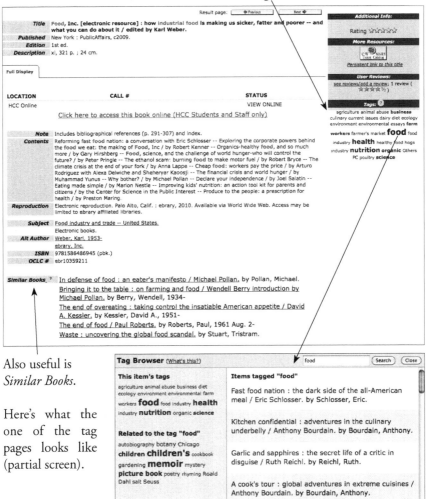

Also useful is *Similar Books*.

Here's what the one of the tag pages looks like (partial screen).

The final word

Searching in the library catalog is becoming more and more like searching the Internet—but without all the pop-ups, viruses, broken links, etc. It tends to have fewer images, so it's less graphically pleasing. But don't you have enough images everywhere else in your browsing life? In short, the library catalog is an extremely effective, efficient way to find quality sources for your papers.

chapter 10

DATABASE RESEARCH

Knowing a great deal is not the same as being smart;
intelligence is not information alone but also judgment,
the manner in which information is collected and used.

~ Carl Sagan

Imagine, for a moment, that you're a fifty-year-old librarian.

When you first started your job, in 1990, the library subscribed to thirty or so popular magazines, ten or fifteen scholarly journals, and a handful of newspapers. The faculty were always asking you to buy new books and subscribe to more academic journals, but it just wasn't in the budget. Also, especially with the periodicals (magazines, journals, newspapers), it was a lot of paper, and the room where you stored it all was just about full.

Fortunately, you also had microfilm and microfiche, those little rolls of film that had tiny pictures of tens of thousands of periodical pages. That system worked, to a degree. But students rarely seemed willing to go to the trouble of finding the right box of films, spooling the film into the giant machines—as big as ovens, and often just as hot—and then trying to read the dimly lit articles.

And then came the digital revolution. All that paper and film was suddenly reduced to digitized bits and stored someplace you never had to think about (or organize), called a database. The best part? People could access it by computer from anywhere in the world.

Now, in 2011, these databases hold more than *one hundred million* articles, as well as images and other research materials.

These databases have everything from a recent *Newsweek* magazine commentary on the death of Osama bin Laden . . .

. . . to *New York Times* editorials from 1860 discussing the possiblity of a Lincoln presidency.

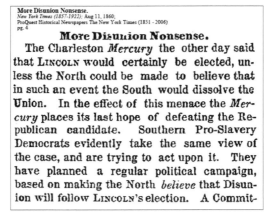

The databases are an amazing storehouse of valuable research materials. And yet very few students take advantage of them. Why?

The simplest reason is that—at least compared to the Internet—databases are harder to find and more challenging to use, at least at first.

WHAT IS A DATABASE?

A database is a collection of articles from magazines, newspapers, encyclopedias, and scholarly journals. Some databases are general, like the one called "General OneFile," where I found that *Newsweek* article. Others are more specialized, like the *New York Times* Historical database, where the Lincoln editorial came from. There are databases devoted just to nursing, education, veterinary medicine and many other fields. Generally, databases are available only by subscription, and in fact your college pays a considerable amount of money so that you can have access to these materials.

HOW DO YOU GET TO THE DATABASES?

Most college students will get to the databases via their college library's web page, which means first going to the college homepage. From there, the method of accessing the databases will vary. Below I demonstrate how it works at my college. If your college's site is confusing, ask a reference librarian for directions.

Go to your college's home page and click on **Library**.

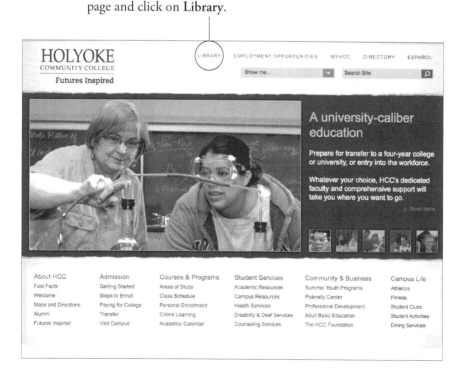

Once you're at the Library homepage, choose **Find Resources** or . . .

. . . Databases and Journals.

I recommend starting with *General Databases (Popular)*. For more scholarly research, try the *Scholarly & Academic* option.

Note also that you can search by field; this may be useful in future courses.

The databases listed on the screen below may be different, so if you don't find the one you want, scroll down the page to see the full list.

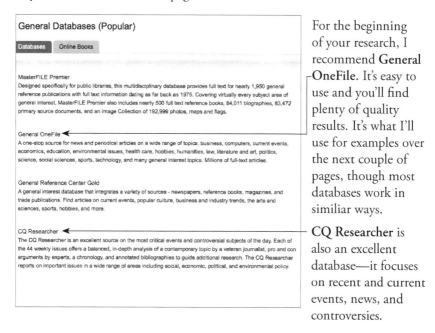

For the beginning of your research, I recommend **General OneFile**. It's easy to use and you'll find plenty of quality results. It's what I'll use for examples over the next couple of pages, though most databases work in similar ways.

CQ Researcher is also an excellent database—it focuses on recent and current events, news, and controversies.

A BASIC DATABASE SEARCH

First, switch to **Advanced Search**.

Sometimes it's helpful to search **entire document**.

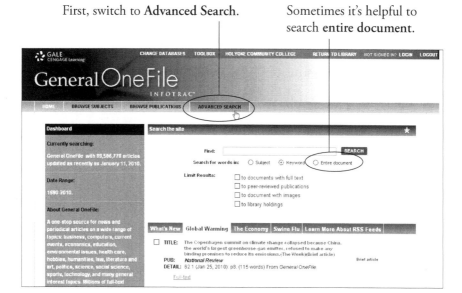

To begin, I'll try putting the terms *industrial food* in the search fields. I tried a few different variations, including putting each word in a separate field, and including the word economy (as I did in previous chapters), but this combination worked best. The lesson? Experiment.

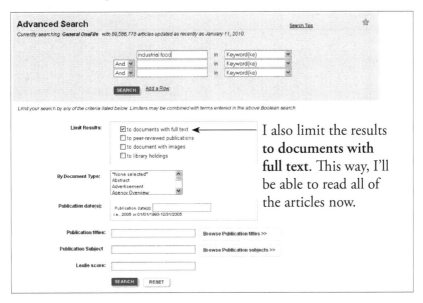

I also limit the results **to documents with full text**. This way, I'll be able to read all of the articles now.

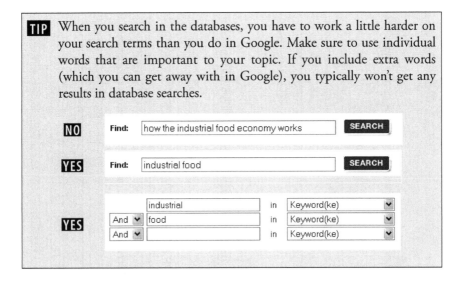

TIP When you search in the databases, you have to work a little harder on your search terms than you do in Google. Make sure to use individual words that are important to your topic. If you include extra words (which you can get away with in Google), you typically won't get any results in database searches.

Here are the results. First, notice that they are organized by tabs, and that the "default" is to academic journals. If you're at the beginning of the research process, you'd probably be better off with magazines. Also make note of the number of results, in this case 1124 for magazines. That's probably too many.

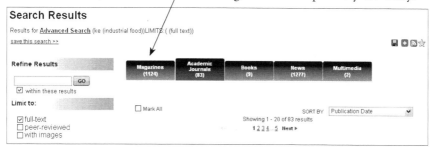

I decided to limit the search by adding the word *economy*. This reduced the results to a manageable number (38).

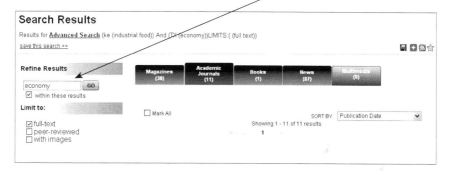

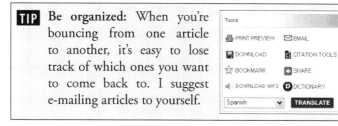

TIP Usually, your search results will be organized by publication date—in other words, they'll list the most recent articles first. Often it's useful to change this so that results are ordered by *Relevance* instead. Use the pull-down menu on the right side of the screen.

TIP **Be organized:** When you're bouncing from one article to another, it's easy to lose track of which ones you want to come back to. I suggest e-mailing articles to yourself.

The article below was the fifth result for magazines. I chose it for two reasons. First, I like the title because it expresses a strong viewpoint. (Click on it to read the article.) Second, I'm familiar with this magazine, *Mother Jones*, and know that it's a reliable source.

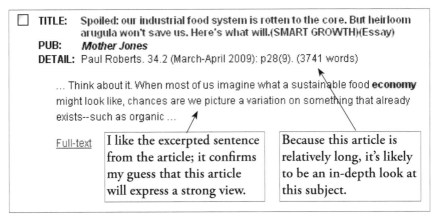

TITLE: Spoiled: our industrial food system is rotten to the core. But heirloom arugula won't save us. Here's what will.(SMART GROWTH)(Essay)
PUB: *Mother Jones*
DETAIL: Paul Roberts. 34.2 (March-April 2009): p28(9). (3741 words)

... Think about it. When most of us imagine what a sustainable food economy might look like, chances are we picture a variation on something that already exists--such as organic ...

Full-text

I like the excerpted sentence from the article; it confirms my guess that this article will express a strong view.

Because this article is relatively long, it's likely to be an in-depth look at this subject.

SEARCHING NEWSPAPERS

If you're researching a topic that's current and newsworthy, you might want to search a newspaper database. The most powerful newspaper database is LexisNexis, which is not always easy to use but does have a huge number of articles from around the world (and not just newspapers). You might also want to look back at Chapter 2 for a review of the types of writing found in newspapers.

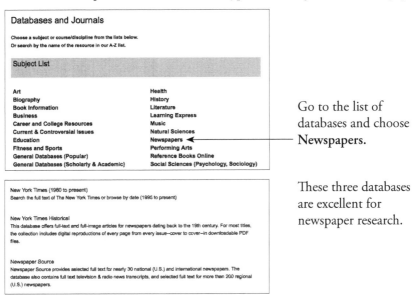

Databases and Journals

Choose a subject or course/discipline from the lists below.
Or search by the name of the resource in our A-Z list.

Subject List

Art
Biography
Book Information
Business
Career and College Resources
Current & Controversial Issues
Education
Fitness and Sports
General Databases (Popular)
General Databases (Scholarly & Academic)

Health
History
Literature
Learning Express
Music
Natural Sciences
Newspapers ◄
Performing Arts
Reference Books Online
Social Sciences (Psychology, Sociology)

Go to the list of databases and choose **Newspapers.**

New York Times (1980 to present)
Search the full text of The New York Times or browse by date (1995 to present)

New York Times Historical
This database offers full-text and full-image articles for newspapers dating back to the 19th century. For most titles, the collection includes digital reproductions of every page from every issue--cover to cover--in downloadable PDF files.

Newspaper Source
Newspaper Source provides selected full text for nearly 30 national (U.S.) and international newspapers. The database also contains full text television & radio news transcripts, and selected full text for more than 200 regional (U.S.) newspapers.

These three databases are excellent for newspaper research.

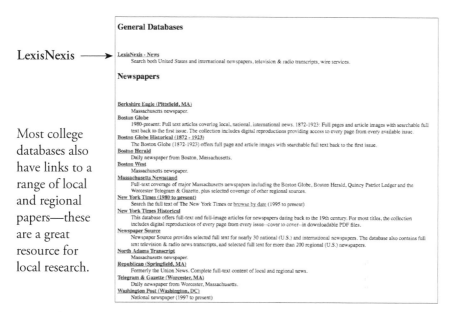

LexisNexis

Most college
databases also
have links to a
range of local
and regional
papers—these
are a great
resource for
local research.

Here's the basic LexisNexis search page. You can generally use the same search terms as in previous database (but not Google) searches. On the next page are a few useful ways to narrow a search using tools on this page.

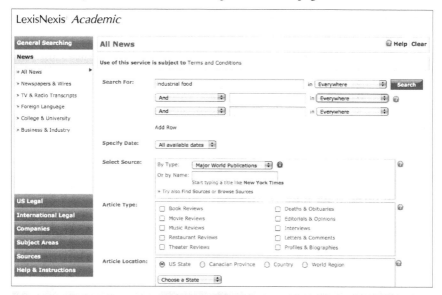

TIP Brainstorm a list of possible keywords (food, industrial, economy, agriculture, organic, sustainable, grocery store, supermarket, etc.) before you even start your search.

If you want only the latest
information on your topic,
choose a recent time window.
For this research, a five-
year window seemed more
appropriate because otherwise
the results might be too limited.

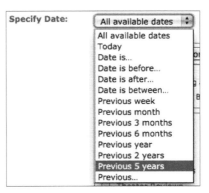

Narrowing the type of source is
a good idea too—LexisNexis is
best for searching newspapers,
so it's a good idea to limit it to
this function. (Other databases
discussed earlier in the chapter
are better at magazine searches.)

If you want to find opinions on your topic (rather than articles that simply
report news events), check the box for *Editorials & Opinions*.

Here are the first six (of 94) articles from this search.

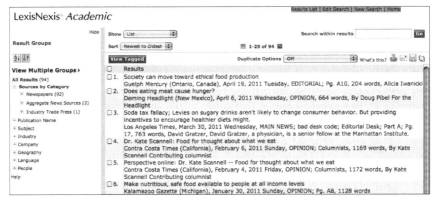

Also, rather than reading through all 94 of the results, you might use the menu on the left side of the screen to see which newspapers published the articles. Maybe you want something from a major newspaper, or from a paper that's near you (on the original search page you could have searched a specific newspaper). Clicking on the newspaper name takes you to the articles from that paper.

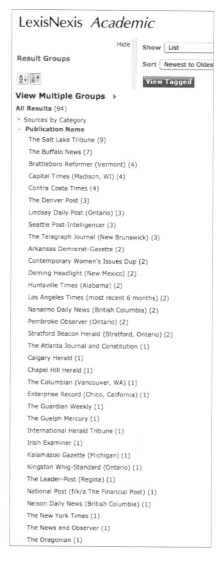

You can also narrow your results by using the *Search within results* function (top right corner of page). Using Michael Pollan's last name here brought the number of article down from 92 to ten. Many of those ten would make excellent sources because they are so specific to the subject matter of this research.

A more advanced way to search in LexisNexis is to use the pull-down menus that control where the database will search for your terms. The default is *Everywhere*.

Let's say that part of your paper will focus specifically on the role of supermarkets in the industrialization of food. Add the keyword *supermarket* to the second search field, and then use the pull-down menu to change *Everywhere* to *At Least 5 Occurrences*. Now, LexisNexis will only give results where the word supermarket is mentioned at least five times.

This more focused search returned 32 results, many of which look promising. I chose the two below because they sound controversial, and because they're both relatively long (the first is about 1200 words; the second is over 3300 words), which suggests that they'll go into some depth. (It's simply a coincidence that they're both from newspapers in England; most of the other articles were from the U.S.)

> ☐ 5. Comment & Debate: Be honest - supermarkets have made our lives better: Yes, the big chains need their excesses to be kept in check, but self-satisfied opponents overlook their social benefits
> The Observer (England), February 17, 2008, OBSERVER COMMENT PAGES; Pg. 29, 1206 words, Jay Rayner

> ☐ 18. What happened to REAL FOOD?; Vegetables without any vitamins, substandard meat and organic apples that won't keep the doctor at bay. No wonder chronic illness is rife. In this shocking new report, we reveal how the true cost of modern food production is 21st-century malnutrition...
> Daily Mail (London), February 21, 2006 Tuesday, ED 1ST 04; Pg. 38, 3316 words, GRAHAM HARVEY

> **TIP** When it comes to database searches, the single most important thing you can do is experiment. I've barely begun to describe what these databases can do—start clicking on things and find out. . . .

CHOOSING THE RIGHT DATABASE

General Interest, Not Exclusively Scholarly

General OneFile	These databases have many articles from general interest, nonacademic magazines such *Time,* *Newsweek, U.S. News and World Report,* etc., dating back to 1980 (1975 for MasterFile).
MasterFILE Premier	

Issues and Controversies	Here you'll find up-to-date information on a broad range of recent issues. These databases are useful if you're writing a persuasive or argumentative essay on a topic of current interest such as affirmative action, salary caps for professional sports, gay rights, and so on. Start here if you're trying to choose a topic for an argumentative paper.
CQ Researcher	

LexisNexis (newspapers)	These databases give you access to back issues of many daily newspapers from across the country and around the world. There are also more localized newspaper databases available; here in Massachusetts, for example, we have a database devoted specifically to the *Boston Globe,* the *Boston Herald,* and a number of smaller, local papers.
Newspaper Source	
New York Times Historical	

More specialized, more scholarly

Academic OneFile	These databases have a good mix of general-interest articles from popular magazines, but they also have the academic journals that you'll need to use for more advanced writing assignments. If your professor requires sources from "peer-reviewed" journals, this is where you should be looking.
Academic Search Premier	
ProQuest Research Library	

Specialized databases (by field)

Check your library's holdings. Many libraries subscribe to specialized databases in nursing, business, literature, law, and many other fields.

chapter 11

MLA DOCUMENTATION

He is wise who knows the sources of knowledge—who knows who has written and where it is to be found.

~ A.A. Hodge

Why do your teachers care so much about documentation?

If you understand why documentation is important to academic work, you're more likely to do it accurately in your papers—and avoid a charge of plagiarism. Documenting your sources serves two purposes: First, it allows readers to know which information or ideas belong to you and which are the product of your research. Second, it enables readers to find those sources and examine them on their own.

Let's say that your paper has been published and a student named Sebastian is reading it; he's intrigued by some of the research you did, particularly one section where you quote someone who talks about homophobia among college sports fans. He sees that the author of the article is Wahl, and now he's curious to read the entire article. If you've done the documentation adequately, Jim should easily be able to find the article (or book, or video, or whatever your source might be). This way, he can enter the "conversation" with his own writing—by reading your paper and then by reading some of your sources to see if he comes to different conclusions about them.

When do you need to document?

You need to document your source any time you use an idea or piece of information that is not yours. If you don't document your sources properly, you may be accused of plagiarism (see Chapter 7).

When do you *not* need to document?

You don't need to cite "common knowledge," which includes strictly factual information that can be found in a number of different sources. For example, if you were writing a paper about Ireland and wanted to mention that the famine happened between 1845 and 1850, you wouldn't need to document that fact (it's widely available as a "fact" and not disputed). If, on the other hand, you read a researcher who asserts that the famine did not affect Ireland's Blasket Islands because the Islanders had a diet that was less reliant on potatoes, then you *would* need to document that. (You may notice that a key difference is whether or not a particular piece of information is open to dispute or different interpretations. Anything that can be disputed or interpreted needs to be documented.)

How do you do it?

It depends on what kind of paper you're writing—because researchers in different fields follow different rules.

In English, for example, you'll use MLA (Modern Language Association), which is what this chapter covers; in psychology and other social sciences, it's called APA (American Psychological Association); in history and other fields, it's Chicago; for most of the sciences, it's CSE (Council of Science Editors).

All four systems have some common features, so learning MLA should help you adapt to those other documentation styles.

Do the two-step.

Documenting your sources properly is a two-step process. Within your paper, you make a quick reference to the source, called an in-text citation. At the end of the paper you provide complete information for all of your sources—this is the works-cited page.

MLA Documentation Directory

IN-TEXT CITATIONS

When I say "in-text," I mean *your* text, the essay you're writing. For the examples here, pretend that these are sentences you would write in your paper. Pay attention to punctuation, spacing, and formatting.

BASIC RULES

Important note: These are the basic rules for in-text citations. Because I'm using a *print* source (an actual magazine that I have held in my hand), I need to include page numbers for my citations. This rule does *not* apply to sources that you use electronically—see *Citing Internet and database sources* on page 156.

I'll use a *Sports Illustrated* article about abusive sports fans as an example. The following sentence appears on page 42.

> What's more, the popularity of social-networking websites such as Facebook and MySpace has made college athletes and their personal information far more accessible to the public, especially if the athletes are naive when it comes to, say, posting compromising photos of themselves or accepting friend requests from strangers.

I like this idea, so I decide to use it in my paper. I put it in my own words:

> **Fans now know more about players, especially their personal lives, in part because many players have Facebook and MySpace pages.**

But this isn't my idea. *I* didn't come to this conclusion from interviewing players or from looking up their pages on my own. Grant Wahl did. Also, I'm borrowing, in a sense, the connection that Wahl is making—that there is a "cause and effect" relationship between the Web pages and the fact that fans feel a greater sense of

"access" to the players. Both the information and the connection *belong to* Wahl; they are his "intellectual property." So, I can't pretend as if I thought of it myself; I have to give Wahl credit. Remember, it doesn't matter that I put the idea in my own words—if I don't give Grant Wahl credit for it, it's plagiarism (see Chapter 7). By the way, would the last user of MySpace please turn out the lights when you're finished?

Important: No matter how you identify the "source" (usually the author), it must correspond with a works-cited entry; in other words, you must have a works-cited entry that begins **Wahl, Grant.**

There are two ways to give Wahl credit:

Method #1: Name the source in the sentence

This is the preferred method for citing a source. Use Grant Wahl's name in a signal phrase (see pages 104–9 for more on these) and put the page number inside paretheses at the end of the sentence.

> **Grant Wahl concludes that fans now know more about players, especially their personal lives, in part because many players have Facebook and MySpace pages (42).**

Note: You only write the author's full name the first time you refer to him. After that, it would just be the last name: "Wahl concludes that fans. . . ."

Method #2: Don't name the source in the sentence

If you don't name the source in your sentence via a signal phrase, you must do so in the parenthetical reference at the end of the sentence. Many professors prefer that students avoid this citation method; check with your professor.

> **Fans now know more about players, especially their personal lives, in part because many players have Facebook and MySpace pages (Wahl 42).**
> ↑
>   Note: There's no comma between the last
>   name and the page number.

The two methods above work the same using a *direct quotation* (the writer's exact words, in his or her order):

IN-TEXT CITATIONS

> Wahl observes that fans can learn a great deal from players' Facebook or MySpace pages, particularly if the players post "compromising photos of themselves or [accept] friend requests from strangers" (42).

Or:

> Fans can learn a great deal from players' Facebook or MySpace pages, particularly if the players post "compromising photos of themselves or [accept] friend requests from strangers" (Wahl 42).

Note how the end of the sentence works; the order of these elements is important. First, close the quotes, and then type a space, then the parentheses for the citation information, then the period.

Citing Internet and database sources

These sources are easy to document because in most cases you can simply eliminate page numbers in your citations. For example, let's say that you found that *Sports Illustrated* article by Grant Wahl online or in a database.

The preferred method is to name the author in your sentence:

> Grant Wahl concludes that fans now know more about players, especially their personal lives, in part because many players have Facebook and MySpace pages.

As with the print examples mentioned earlier, you can also write the sentence without mentioning Wahl's name, though you do then need to put his name inside the parentheses:

> Fans now know more about players, especially their personal lives, in part because many players have Facebook and MySpace pages (Wahl).

Using brackets

You might have noticed that I used [brackets] around the word *accept* in the quotation at the top of the page. That's because I changed the word slightly—in the original, the word is *accepting*. If I had written *accepting*, it would have made my sentence grammatically awkward. (Actually, it would have been more than awkward; it would have been wrong.) Often, when you're quoting part of a sentence, the exact words of the quotation don't quite flow properly within your sentence, typically because of a verb. Change as little as you can, and let your reader know which word or words have been changed by putting them inside brackets.

Integrating material into your sentences

Notice that in all of my sample sentences I have *integrated* the quoted or paraphrased material into my sentences. You need to do this too. Make the material that you refer to *a part of* your sentence, and make sure that the sentence you end up with reads smoothly and is grammatically correct. Refer to Chapter 7 for additional guidelines.

COMPLICATIONS TO THE BASIC RULES

Generally, the above examples will get you through the vast majority of in-text citations. But there's a good chance you'll have to deal with some variations.

Important note: In most of the examples that follow, I use sources that appeared in print, which means that I include page numbers. If you're applying these rules to an Internet or non-print source, just eliminate the page number; also eliminate any punctuation that comes immediately before the page number. For example, the citation below would be: ("Over the Top").

No author listed

Pretend that the *Sports Illustrated* article did not have an author listed; in that case, use a shortened form (if it needs to be shortened) of the title of the article, inside quotation marks:

> Fans can learn a great deal from players' Facebook or MySpace pages, particularly if the players post "compromising photos of themselves or [accept] friend requests from strangers" ("Over the Top," 42).

> *if you read it online:*   from strangers" ("Over the Top").

Note: How you abbreviate the title is up to you, but be sure to use the first word (unless it's *a, an* or *the*)—because this is the word a reader would be looking for on the works-cited page. For some reason, MLA says you need a comma between the title and page number (but you don't after an author's name—go figure).

IN-TEXT CITATIONS

Two or three authors

For the sake of simplicity, let's pretend that the *Sports Illustrated* article was written by two or three authors. First, let's add a second author, James Gillen:

> Wahl and Gillen conclude that fans now know more about players, especially their personal lives, in part because many players have Facebook and MySpace pages (42).

Or:

> Fans can learn a great deal from players' Facebook or MySpace pages, particularly if the players post "compromising photos of themselves or [accept] friend requests from strangers" (Wahl and Gillen 42).

If there had been a third author (let's pretend she's named Delia Morlund), and she were listed third, your parenthetical citation would look like this:

> Wahl, Gillen, and Morlund conclude that fans now know more about players, especially their personal lives, in part because many players have Facebook and MySpace pages (42).

Or:

> Fans can learn a great deal from players' Facebook or MySpace pages, particularly if the players post "compromising photos of themselves or [accept] friend requests from strangers" (Wahl, Witkin, and Morlund 42).

Page numbers: Remember that if you found this source online or in databases, you would simply eliminate the page numbers.

Four or more authors

Let's further assume that the above example added a fourth author, Seth Jackson. If you name the authors in your sentence, you use the first author's name only, followed by *et al.*, which is Latin for *and others*.

> Grant Wahl et al. conclude that fans now know more about players, especially their personal lives, in part because many players have Facebook and MySpace pages (42).

Or, if you don't want to name the authors in the sentence:

> Fans can learn a great deal from players' Facebook or MySpace pages, particularly if the players post "compromising photos of themselves or [accept] friend requests from strangers" (Wahl et al. 42).

Page numbers: Remember that if you found this source online or in databases, you would simply eliminate the page numbers.

Quoting someone who's being quoted

Yes, this is tricky—but not all that uncommon. In this example, I'll quote from the final sentence of this paragraph, from the same *Sports Illustrated* article:

> Why is homophobia so prevalent today? While Jack Aiello, a psychology professor at Rutgers, cautions that racism still hasn't disappeared—after all, he had a ground-zero view last year of the fallout from Don Imus's derogatory remarks about the mostly black Rutgers women's basketball team—he says that today's college sports venues can be flash points for homophobic behavior. "I've seen in the last 10 to 15 years a continuing elevation in the visibility of gays and lesbians on campuses, and greater visibility brings the potential for reactions by majority groups," Aiello says. "People who have strong feelings of opposition are more likely to demonstrate them, and where's a venue to do that? In a macho sports-arena environment."

Remember two things, and you'll get it right.

First, mention the person you're quoting (Aiello, in this case) in your sentence, and use his or her full name. Then, in your parenthetical reference, use the abbreviation *qtd. in* (for "quoted in") before the author of the article—because that's what your reader will be looking for on the works-cited page if she wants to find the article.

> Psychologist Jack Aiello calls this the "macho sports-arena environment" (qtd. in Wahl 42).

Page numbers: Remember that if you found this source online or in databases, you would simply eliminate the page numbers.

IN-TEXT CITATIONS

Work in an anthology

An anthology is a collection of essays, stories, or poems by many different authors. Many textbooks used in English courses are anthologies.
For the in-text citation, you don't really need to worry about the fact that the book is an anthology. Just be sure that your citation refers to the actual writer of the story, poem or essay—not the editor(s) of the anthology.

> Jane Smiley suggests that the problem may have its source in "the ubiquity of sugar" (328).

Or:

> Perhaps the problem is "the ubiquity of sugar" (Smiley 328).

When you do the works-cited entry, you'll need to know the name of Smiley's essay, "Reflections on a Lettuce Wedge," the name of the anthology, *The Writer's Presence*, and that it's edited by Donald McQuade and Robert Atwan, as well as other publication information. See **Book with an editor** and **Work in an anthology** in the works-cited part of this chapter for more information.

Long quotation (also known as block quotation)

If you quote something that is four lines or longer, format it as follows:

Your writing, to introduce the quotation.

By examining the marketing practices of mainstream grocery stores, Pollan reveals the preeminence of quantification:

Block quotation, indented 1 inch from left. The right margin stays the same. It's double-spaced just like the rest of your text.

> Just look at the typical newspaper ad for a supermarket. The sole quality on display here is actually a quantity: tomatoes $0.69 a pound; ground chuck $1.09 a pound; eggs $0.99 a dozen—special this week. Is there any other category of product sold on such a reductive basis? (136)

Your writing, to comment on the quotation.

By highlighting the focus on price and quantity, Pollan exposes a peculiar—and potentially dangerous—complicity between consumers and grocery businesses.

Also note that the block quotation ends with the page number where you found the quotation, inside parentheses and *after* the punctuation mark.

IN-TEXT CITATIONS

Formatting a Block Quotation

If you quote something four or more lines long, format it as follows. If you're using an earlier version of Word, see appendix, pages 238-9.

1. Start by highlighting the text you're quoting. Then, click on the **View** tab.

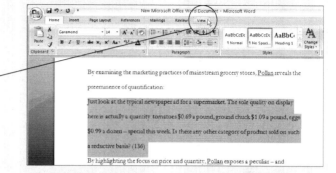

2. Check the **Ruler** box.

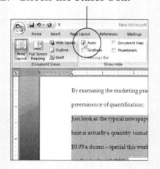

3. This little gadget is made up of three parts. You want to click on and hold the bottom one, the very small square, then drag it 1/2 inch to the right.

Note: If you let your cursor hover over the boxes, it will display the function; when it says **Hanging Indent**, you've got the right one.

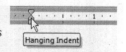

4. This is how it should look when you're finished.

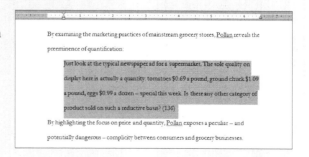

Organization or group as author

It's easiest to name the organization in your sentence:

> According to the Modern Language Association, "The study of the most popular languages—Spanish, French, and German—continues to grow and represents more than 70 percent of language enrollments."

But you can also do it the other way:

> Recent research suggests that students continue to study the most traditionally popular languages; more than 70 percent of students are taking Spanish, French, and German (Modern Language Association).

Note: I did not include a page number for either citation because I found the quotation on the organization's Website.

Author who wrote two or more books (that you cite in your paper)

Let's say that I read two books by Michael Pollan (*The Omnivore's Dilemma* and *In Defense of Food*), and I'm using them both as sources in my paper. So that there's no confusion about which book I'm referring to, I need to provide a shortened reference to the book inside the parentheses.

> Michael Pollan asserts that both our civilization and our "food system" are "strictly organized on industrial lines" (*Omnivore* 201).

Or:

> It has been argued that both our civilization and our "food system" are "strictly organized on industrial lines" (Pollan, *Omnivore* 201).

Note: If I had been using an article rather than a book, I would have still used a shortened form of the title, but it would be inside quotation marks, not italicized.

Two authors with same last name

It doesn't happen very often, but it does happen. If you refer to the author within the sentence, use the first and last name each time.

> Christopher Alexander describes the problem this way: "A complex of buildings with no center is like a man without a head" (486).

Or:

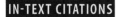

One architectural theorist describes the problem this way: "A complex of buildings with no center is like a man without a head" (C. Alexander 486).

Two or more authors in the same sentence

Put the parenthetical citation immediately after the information you're citing from each author.

It has been said that heightened awareness of the sources of our food connects people to their "agricultural roots" (Smiley 437), or even to their "feral past" (Winckler 28).

Two authors who make the same point

Again, this will happen only rarely. Your citation should name both authors, separated by a semi-colon.

(Pollan 486; Jones 54).

Citing a Kindle, Nook, or other e-reader

Provide more information than you usually would (at least until the e-readers and MLA come to see agreement); many scholars are including some reference to the chapter in which source material appeared:

In Chapter 10, "Grass," Michael Pollan asserts that both our civilization and our "food system" are "strictly organized on industrial lines."

WORKS-CITED ENTRIES

FIRST, A FEW UNIVERSAL GUIDELINES

Don't obsess. I should probably be telling you how incredibly important it is that you do all of this exactly right, all the time. But I think you'd be better off with more reasonable advice, namely to be conscientious and make a good effort to get all of this right, but also to remember that even professionals make mistakes.

In short, do the best you can, but don't obsess over this stuff. If you've been madly flipping through this book for ten minutes, trying to determine whether you need a comma or a period after an editor's name, you're obsessing. Use your judgment, make a choice, and move on.

Capitalization

I admit it—it doesn't make much sense that you're supposed to capitalize titles "properly" when the journal or magazine article you're citing hasn't done so. I'm not sure why this happens, but all you really need to know is that it's your job to do it right whether your source does or not.

Always capitalize   the first and last words of the title
nouns, verbs, adjectives, and adverbs

Do *not* capitalize   prepositions: of, on, around, behind, and many more
articles: a, an, the
conjunctions: and, but, or, for, nor, so, yet
infinitive: to

So, even though that *Sports Illustrated* article looks like this (Over The Top) in the database, you would write, Over the Top.

Long titles

Sometimes, particularly with newspaper and magazine articles, you'll come across some very long titles. Or at least they look that way; in many cases, what you're seeing, particularly in the case of databases, is a headline and also a sub-headline.

You have to use your judgment about what's really the title and what's not, but I do have a few suggestions. Use the whole title, even if it's long, when it's the title of a book or an article in a scholarly journal. Use a shortened version of the title when it's very, very long and/or the second part appears to be a complete sentence. Whenever possible, it helps to look at the original (or a PDF) so you can see the original formatting—then it's often obvious what the *real* title is.

Author names

The basic rule is that you reverse the order of the first author's name, but leave the others in usual order.

One author: Smith, Doug K.
    If Smith didn't have a middle initial: Smith, Doug.

WORKS-CITED ENTRIES

Two authors: Smith, Doug K., and Jean T. Philips.

> If Smith didn't have a middle initial: Smith, Doug, and Jean T. Philips.

Three authors: Smith, Doug K., Jean T. Philips, and Bertha Q. McBride.

> If Smith didn't have a middle initial: Smith, Doug, Jean T. Philips, and Bertha Q. McBride.

Four authors: Smith, Doug K., et al. (Et al. is an abbreviation for *and others*.)

> If Smith didn't have a middle initial: Smith, Doug, et al.

Abbreviations of months

Most months are abbreviated; here's how all of them should look:

Jan.	Feb.	Mar.	Apr.	May	June
July	Aug.	Sept.	Oct.	Nov.	Dec.

Abbreviations of publishers' names

If the publisher is listed as, for example, The Macmillan Company, you would simply write Macmillan.

For academic journals, their publisher is often a university press. If, for example, it's Harvard University Press, you would abbreviate it Harvard UP (no period— but my sentence now needs one).

Spaces

With some of the examples on the following pages, it's hard to tell where you should have a space. You always have a space after any mark of punctuation (comma, period, colon, semi-colon); also rememember that between each "part" of an entry (like, for example, between a magazine name and its date of publication), you always need a space.

HOW THE REST OF THIS CHAPTER IS ORGANIZED

First question: Are you holding the source in your hand?

Before the Internet age, this would have been a dumb question. Now, it marks the great dividing line in documentation. Is your source an actual physical thing you're holding in your hand, or is it something you're looking at on a computer screen?

WORKS-CITED ENTRIES

If you're holding it in your hand, it's a print source. If you're looking at it on a screen, it's either an Internet source or a database source. There are also a few other, less common source types that don't exactly fit into one of those three categories. That makes four "categories" of sources, and it gives the rest of this chapter its organization: print, Internet, database, other.

Note: Because this book is intended to be a quick guide to the most common issues facing first-year writers, there are some sources that I'm not including here. If there's something I don't cover that you need to know how to cite, I highly recommend the Purdue University site, *The Owl at Purdue*. Do a Google search for *Purdue Owl MLA* to find it.

PRINT SOURCES — BOOKS

Book with one author

Author's Last Name, First Name. *Book Title: Book Subtitle**. City of Publication: Publisher, Year of Publication. Medium.

* Include subtitle after a colon, and always capitalize the first word after the colon.

Pollan, Michael. *The Omnivore's Dilemma: A Natural History of Four Meals*. New York: Penguin, 2006. Print.

NOTE: The second line of the entry is indented. (See page 184 for how to do a "hanging indent.")

Book with two, three, four or more authors

See guidelines on pages 164–5 for how to write additional author names.

Book with an editor

The editor is listed as the "main" author for the sake of the works-cited entry. Keep in mind, though, that if you cite particular essays or stories from within this book, you need an entry for each of these authors too. Yes, this is a little confusing. See also the guideline for *Work from an anthology* later in this chapter.

As far as the works-cited entry goes, this is just like any other book, with the simple addition of the abbreviation *eds.* for the editors. If there had been only one editor, the abbreviation would be ed.

> Hofstadter, Albert, and Richard Kuhns, eds. *Philsophies of Art and*
> *Beauty: Selected Readings in Aesthetics from Plato to Heidegger.*
> Chicago: University of Chicago Press, 1964. Print.

Book that lists an edition

Many books (textbooks, especially) are republished with the same title but new content. If your book has an edition listed, it will probably be noticeable on the cover and/or the spine. In the works-cited entry, put the edition after the title.

> McQuade, Donald, and Robert Atwan, eds. *The Writer's Presence: A Pool*
> *of Readings.* 5th ed. Boston: Bedford / St. Martin's, 2007. Print.

Two or more books by same author

Use three dashes to indicate a repeat of the author's name. Put each book in alphabetical order (*In* before *Omnivore*).

> Pollan, Michael. *In Defense of Food: An Eater's Manifesto.* New York:
> Penguin, 2008. Print.
> ---. *The Omnivore's Dilemma: A Natural History of Four Meals.* New York:
> Penguin, 2006. Print.

Book by an anonymous author

Don't write Anonymous or Anon. for the author. Just go straight to the title.

> *Primary Colors: A Novel of Politics.* New York: Random House, 2006.
> Print.

WORKS CITED: PRINT

BOOKS

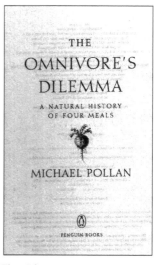

The front cover

Here you should find the full title, though sometimes there's so much additional information on the cover that it can be hard to tell exactly what the title is. When there's a subtitle, it's even more confusing. Looking at the title page can help.

The title page

Title, subtitle, author and publisher—all on one page. (It's not always this straightforward.)

Note: Everything here is capitalized, which you do not want to do in your documentation. See specific guidelines on capitalization on page 164.

The spine

The spine (or edge) of book will usually have the full name of the book (often with subtitle, as in this case) and the author's full name. The spine is also the most reliable place to find the name of the publisher; this case is unusual in that it shows a penguin rather than the name of the publisher, which happens to be . . . Penguin Books.

The copyright page

You will need to look at this page, usually, to find out what year the book was published and what city the publisher is in. This is unfortunate, because there's so much information on this page that it can be difficult to find what you need.

If you look at all the cities listed here, you could easily get confused about the city of publication. It's almost always the first one listed: New York, in this case.

PENGUIN BOOKS
Published by the Penguin Group
Penguin Group (USA) Inc., 375 Hudson Street, New York, New York 10014, U.S.A.
Penguin Group (Canada), 90 Eglinton Avenue East, Suite 700, Toronto,
Ontario, Canada M4P 2Y3 (a division of Pearson Penguin Canada Inc.)
Penguin Books Ltd, 80 Strand, London WC2R 0RL, England
Penguin Ireland, 25 St Stephen's Green, Dublin 2, Ireland (a division of Penguin Books Ltd)
Penguin Group (Australia), 250 Camberwell Road, Camberwell,
Victoria 3124, Australia (a division of Pearson Australia Group Pty Ltd)
Penguin Books India Pvt Ltd, 11 Community Centre, Panchsheel Park, New Delhi – 110 017, India
Penguin Group (NZ), 67 Apollo Drive, Rosedale, North Shore 0745,
Auckland, New Zealand (a division of Pearson New Zealand Ltd)
Penguin Books (South Africa) (Pty) Ltd, 24 Sturdee Avenue,
Rosebank, Johannesburg 2196, South Africa

Penguin Books Ltd, Registered Offices:
80 Strand, London WC2R 0RL, England

Year of publication presents more complications. Is it 2006 or 2007?

First published in the United States of America by The Penguin Press,
a member of Penguin Group (USA) Inc. 2006
Published in Penguin Books 2007

3 5 7 9 10 8 6 4 2

Go with the year that has the © symbol—in this case, 2006.

Copyright © Michael Pollan, 2006
All rights reserved

THE LIBRARY OF CONGRESS HAS CATALOGED THE HARDCOVER EDITION AS FOLLOWS:
Pollan, Michael.
The omnivore's dilemma : a natural history of four meals / Michael Pollan.
p. cm.
Includes bibliographical references and index.
ISBN 1-59420-082-3 (hc.)
ISBN 978-0-14-303858-0 (pbk.)
1. GT2850.P65 2006.   2. Food habits.   3. Food preferences.   I. Title.
GT2850.P65 2006
394.1'2—dc22   2005056557

Printed in the United States of America
DESIGNED BY MARYSARAH QUINN

Except in the United States of America, this book is sold subject to the condition that it shall not, by way of trade or otherwise, be lent, resold, hired out, or otherwise circulated without the publisher's prior consent in any form of binding or cover other than that in which it is published and without a similar condition including this condition being imposed on the subsequent purchaser.

WORKS CITED: PRINT

Book by an organization or group

Start with the name of the organization or group, followed by the book title.

> Modern Language Association. *MLA Style Manual and Guide to Scholarly Publishing*. 3rd ed. New York: Modern Language Association of America, 2008. Print.

Book that has been translated

Start with the person who wrote the book, *not* the translator.

> Barthes, Roland. *The Eiffel Tower and Other Mythologies*. Trans. Richard Howard. New York: Noonday, 1979. Print.

Book that has been reprinted

When citing older literary works (novels, plays, collections of poems or stories), you should include the year that the book was originally published.

> Melville, Herman. *Moby Dick*. 1851. New York: Quality Paperback Book Club, 1996. Print.

Book in more than one volume

After the title, write the volume number that you used; after the year of publication, write the total number of volumes of the book.

> Kelby, Scott. *The Digital Photography Book*. Vol. 2. Berkeley: Peachpit Press, 2008. 2 vols. Print.

Book that has a title within the title

When scholars write about another book, they often include the title of the book in *their* title. Don't italicize the title that appears within their title.

> Brodhead, Richard H., ed. *New Essays on* Moby Dick. Cambride, Mass.: Cambride UP, 1986. Print.

WORKS CITED: PRINT

Encyclopedia or dictionary

In most reference books (such as encyclopedias and dictionaries), no author is listed, so you simply start with the title of the entry. After the name of the book, include the edition (abbreviated as below) and the year. If there *is* an author listed, then put that first. But I have a feeling you knew that.

"Botox." *The New Encyclopædia Britannica*. 15th ed. 2003. Print.

PRINT SOURCES — PERIODICALS (Magazines, Newspapers, Journals)

We call these periodicals because they are published *periodically*, meaning: on a schedule. The schedule could be daily, weekly, monthly, bi-monthly. But whatever it is, it comes again and again, at times that readers can count on. You should know how to identify three types of periodicals, and the easiest way to do so is by their publication frequency (how often they publish):

- **MAGAZINES** like *Time, Newsweek, Sports Illustrated* and *The New Yorker* publish weekly; others bi-weekly (every two weeks); many monthly—*Esquire, The Atlantic Monthly, Harper's*, etc. Possible confusion: Weekly magazines will have a publication date that looks exactly like a daily newspaper: November 19, 2003. See next entry for help with this.

- **NEWSPAPERS** are, typically, published daily, so their date of publication will always be a particular day: October 1, 1996. If you're trying to figure out if a publication is a newspaper or a weekly magazine, remember that you've heard of most weekly magazines. Also, newspapers tend to have names that give them away: they begin with the name of a city, and most include words like Post, Gazette, Times, Globe, Herald, Tribune, etc., in their title.

- **JOURNALS** typically, are scholarly publications read by people in specialized fields. They are usually published seasonally, i.e. Spring 2010, and tend to have the words journal or review in their titles, as in *The Hemingway Review*, or *The Journal of Abnormal Psychology*. How do you know that the the *Wall Street Journal* is a newspaper and not a journal? Because journals are not published daily, ever.

WORKS CITED: PRINT

Article in a magazine (print)

> Author's Last Name, First Name. "Title of Article." *Name of Magazine*
> Date: Page range. Medium.

> Wahl, Grant. "Over the Top." *Sports Illustrated* 3 Mar. 2008: 40-44.
> Print.

• There's no punctuation after the name of the magazine.
• For weekly and bi-weekly magazines, you need an exact date as shown above; for monthly and bi-monthly magazines, you only need the month and year.
• Abbreviate months as shown on page 165.
• For two, three, four or more authors, see pages 164–5.

Article in a newspaper (print)

> Author's Last Name, First Name. "Title of Article." *Name of Newspaper*
> Date: Page range. Medium.

> McCabe, Kathy. "State Board Fines Lynn's Fire Chief over Supervision of
> Wife." *Boston Globe* 21 Dec. 2006: T5. Print.

• There's no punctuation after the name of the newspaper.
• If the article continues on another page, add the plus sign, i.e., T5+.
• Abbreviate months as shown on page 165.
• For two, three, four or more authors, see pages 164–5.

WORKS CITED: PRINT

Editorial in a newspaper (print)

"Title of Editorial." Editorial. *Name of Newspaper* Date: Page range. Medium.

"Snow Days: Hold the Cocoa." Editorial. *Boston Globe* 14 Jan. 2011: A14. Print.

- Generally, editorials will not have an author listed.
- There's no punctuation after the name of the newspaper.
- Abbreviate months as shown on page 165.
- For two, three, four or more authors, see pages 164–5.

Article in an academic journal (print)

Author's Last Name, First Name. "Title of Article: Subtitle." *Name of Journal* Volume.Issue (Year): Page range. Medium.

Steinberg, Shirley R., and Joe L. Kincheloe. "Privileged and Getting Away with It: The Cultural Studies of White, Middle-Class Youth." *Studies in the Literary Imagination* 31.1 (1998): 103-27. Print.

- Most articles in academic journals include subtitles, which you almost always should include in your works-cited entry (see guidelines for long titles on page 164).
- There's no punctuation after the name of the journal.
- Format volume and issue numbers correctly, as shown above; often, these look very different in the source itself: Vol. 31, No. 1, or v31n1, etc.
- For two, three, four or more authors, see pages 164–5.

WORKS CITED: PRINT

Work in an anthology—a book with many different authors (print)

Many textbooks, particularly in English classes, are *anthologies*; an anthology is a collection of works (essays, stories, poems, and/or plays) written by many different authors. If you're using one essay from an anthology here's how you cite it:

> Author's Last Name, First Name. "Title of Essay." *Name of Book.* Ed.
>
> First Name Last Name. City of Publication: Publisher, Year of
>
> Publication. Page range. Medium.

> Hughes, Langston. "Salvation." *The Writer's Presence: A Pool of Readings.*
>
> Eds. Donald McQuade and Robert Atwan. Boston: Bedford / St.
>
> Martin's, 2007. 163-65. Print.

- This is the guideline for when you're citing only one essay, story, play, or poem from an anthology; if you cite more than one, see the next entry.
- Use Ed. for one editor, Eds. for two or more. The editors' names will be on the front of the book and on the title page.

Two or more works from the same anthology (print)

When you use two different authors from the same anthology, you have to do the works-cited entries very differently. Do a shortened entry for each essay, story, or poem, and also do a full entry for the whole book.

Note: Put each entry on your works-cited page wherever it belongs alphabetically; in other words, these would not be grouped together. See last page of chapter.

Entry for individual essay you read in the anthology	Hughes, Langston. "Salvation." McQuade and Atwan 163-65.
Full entry for whole book	McQuade, Donald, and Robert Atwan, eds. 5th ed. *The Writer's Presence: A Pool of Readings.* Boston: Bedford / St. Martin's, 2007. Print.
Entry for individual essay you read in the anthology	Wolfe, Tom. "Hooking Up." McQuade and Atwan 611-18.

WORKS CITED: PRINT

INTERNET SOURCES

Note that in most cases you need to use the name of the website and the publisher of the site (typically found at the bottom of the page).

The publisher's name is listed after ©2009; in this case, Time Inc.

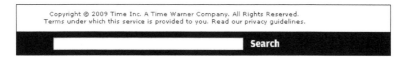

Article in a magazine (online)

This is the guideline you'd use for just about any "article" you find online. It doesn't matter if the publication has a print version or not.

> Author's Last Name, First Name. "Title of Article." *Name of Website.*
>
> Publisher, Date. Medium. Date you accessed article.

> Wahl, Grant. "Over the Top." *SI.com.* Time Inc., 27 Feb. 2008. Web. 19
>
> Sept. 2009.

- If the website seems distinctive from the print version of the magazine, use the website name: *SI.com* rather than *Sports Illustrated;* more often, though, you would write the name without *.com*: *Slate, Salon, Time, Newsweek*, etc.
- Generally, you should not include subtitles for magazine articles (see guidelines for long titles on page 164).
- Abbreviate months as shown on page 165.
- For two, three, four or more authors, see pages 164–5.

WORKS CITED: INTERNET

Article in a newspaper (online)

Author's Last Name, First Name. "Title of Article." *Name of Newspaper.* Publisher, Date. Medium. Date you accessed article.

Pariser, Eli. "When the Internet Thinks It Knows You." *New York Times.* New York Times, 23 May 2011. Web. 23 May 2011.

- Generally, you should not include subtitles for newspaper articles (see guidelines for long titles on page 164).
- Abbreviate months as shown on page 165.
- For two, three, four or more authors, see pages 164–5.

Editorial in a newspaper (online)

"Title of Editorial." Editorial. *Name of Newspaper.* Publisher, Date. Medium. Date you accessed article.

"Snow Days: Hold the Cocoa." Editorial. *Boston Globe.* New York Times, 23 May 2011. Web. 23 May 2011.

- Generally, editorials will not have an author listed.
- Abbreviate months as shown on page 165.

Article in an academic journal (online)

Author's Last Name, First Name. "Title of Article: Subtitle." *Name of Journal* Volume.Issue (Year): Page range. Medium.

Steinberg, Shirley R., and Joe L. Kincheloe. "Privileged and Getting Away with It: The Cultural Studies of White, Middle-Class Youth." *Studies in the Literary Imagination* 31.1 (1998): 103-27. Web. 19 Sept. 2007.

If the journal did not publish a print version, you would not include page numbers. So, above, the end of the entry would look like this:

> *Studies in the Literary Imagination* 31.1 (1998): n. pag. Web. 19
> Sept. 2007.

- Most articles in academic journals include subtitles, which you almost always should include in your works-cited entry (see guidelines for long titles on page 164).
- There's no punctuation after the name of the journal.
- Format volume and issue numbers correctly, as shown above; often, these look very different in the source itself: Vol. 31, No. 1, or v31n1, etc.
- For two, three, four or more authors, see pages 164–5.

Book that you read online

> Author's Last Name, First Name. *Book Title: Book Subtitle*. City of
> Publication: Publisher, Year of Publication. *Name of Site*. Medium.
> Date of access.

> Menasche, Emile D. *Home Studio Clinic: A Musician's Guide to
> Professional Recording*. New York: Hal Leonard, 2007. *Google Books*.
> Web. 24 Dec. 2009.

- Abbreviate months as shown on page 165.
- For two, three, four or more authors, see pages 164–5.

Article with no author (online)

This was an article I found through MSN.com. As with many "news" stories online, there's no author listed. So, start with the article title and proceed as you would with other online entries.

> "911 Caller: Husband Won't Eat Dinner." *MSNBC.com*. MSNBC.com,
> 24 Dec. 2009. Web. 24 Dec. 2009.

- Abbreviate months as shown on page 165.

WORKS CITED: INTERNET

Online page published by group or organization

Name of Organization. "Title of Article." *Name of Website.* Publisher,

Date. Medium. Date you accessed article.

Modern Language Association. "What is MLA Style?" *MLA.org.* Modern

Language Association, 13 Jan. 2009. Web. 24 Dec. 2009.

- With many websites produced by an organization, the name of the organization itself can be listed as the author. Obviously, if there's a person's name listed as the author, use it.
- Abbreviate months as shown on page 165.

Email message

Last Name, First Name (of person who wrote email). "Subject of

Message." Message to Your Name (or name of person who received

the message, if not you). Date of Email. Medium.

Shirk, Zoe. "Re: Further Thoughts on Writing Process." Message to Fred

Cooksey. 25 June 2008. E-mail.

WORKS CITED: INTERNET

Complications—and two important abbreviations

You're likely to encounter two problems with Web pages: there's no obvious date for the page or you can't find a publisher listed. In both cases, use an abbreviation:

N.p. = no publisher   n.d. = no date

Let's take the above example from the MLA site as an example; here's how it would look if there were no publisher:

> Modern Language Association. "What is MLA Style?" *MLA.org.* N.p., 13
> Jan. 2009. Web. 24 Dec. 2009.

And if there were no date:

> Modern Language Association. "What is MLA Style?" *MLA.org.* Modern
> Language Association, n.d. Web. 24 Dec. 2009.

DATABASE SOURCES

Use this guideline if you found the article through a database; most databases require you to sign in, though some may give you direct access if you're on campus. See Chapter 10 for more information.

Article in a magazine or newspaper (database)

> Author's Last Name, First Name. "Title of Article." *Name of Magazine or
> Newspaper* Date: Page range. *Name of Database.* Medium. Date you
> accessed article.

> Wahl, Grant. "Over the Top." *Sports Illustrated* 3 Mar. 2008: 40-
> 44. *Academic OneFile.* Web. 13 June 2008.

- There's no punctuation after the name of the magazine or newspaper.
- Abbreviate months as shown on page 165.
- For two, three, four or more authors, see pages 164–5.

WORKS CITED: DATABASE

Article in an academic journal (database)

Author's Last Name, First Name. "Title of Article." *Name of Journal* Volume.Issue (Year): Page range. *Name of Database*. Medium. Date you accessed article.

Steinberg, Shirley R., and Joe L. Kincheloe. "Privileged and Getting Away with It: The Cultural Studies of White, Middle-Class Youth." *Studies in the Literary Imagination* 31.1 (1998): 103-27. *Academic OneFile*. Web. 19 Sept. 2007.

- Most articles in academic journals include subtitles, which you almost always should include in your works-cited entry (see guidelines for long titles on page 164).
- There's no punctuation after the name of the journal.
- Format volume and issue numbers correctly, as shown above; often, these look very different in the source itself: Vol. 31, No. 1, or v31n1, etc.
- For two, three, four or more authors, see pages 164–5.

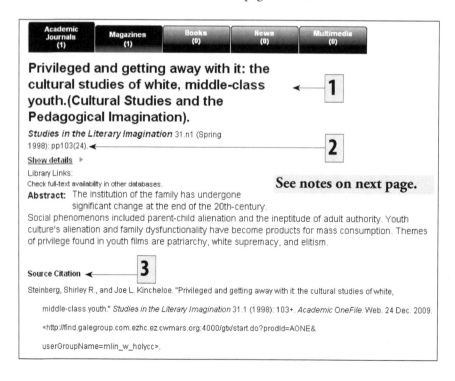

1 The title is not properly capitalized here, and there's extra information inside the parentheses that common sense should tell you not to include.

3 Just so you know, the "citation" provided by the database has numerous errors. It's close, but you should follow my example below.

2 Often the page range will look like this: 103(24). In cases like this, they're telling you what page the article starts on and how long it is; do the math. 103+24 = 127.

OTHER SOURCES

Interview

Use this format when you have personally interviewed someone as a source for your paper; start with person's name, last name first.

Gillen, Claire. Personal interview. 4 July 2011.

Film / DVD

Title of Film. Director. Performers. Name of Studio that produced film, Year of release. Medium.

Inglourious Basterds. Dir. Quentin Tarantino. Perf. Brad Pitt, Diane Kruger, Christoph Waltz, and Eli Roth. Universal Pictures, 2009. Film.

- My example includes performers, but you are not required to include these.
- If you watched the movie on DVD, just change the word *Film* at the end to DVD.

If your essay focuses more on the director, reorder the entry as follows:

Tarantino, Quentin, dir. *Inglourious Basterds*. Perf. Brad Pitt, Diane Kruger, Christoph Waltz, and Eli Roth. Universal Pictures, 2009. Film.

WORKS CITED: OTHER

Television show

If you watched it when it was broadcast, provide name of episode, name of show, network (ABC, NBC, etc.), call letters of the station you watched it on, and city.

"Title of Episode." *Title of Show*. Network. Station you watched it on, City (and state, if needed) of Station. Date show aired. Medium.

"Abed's Uncontrollable Christmas." *Community*. NBC. WWLP, Springfield, MA. 10 Dec. 2010. Television.

• Abbreviate months as shown on page 165.

If you watched it on DVD or in some other form after the original broadcast, follow this form (names of director and writers are optional):

"Title of Episode." *Title of Show*. Writer(s). Director. Publisher. Medium.

"Abed's Uncontrollable Christmas." *Community*. Writ. Dino Stamatopoulos and Dan Harmon. Dir. Duke Johnson. Sony, 2011. DVD.

Radio broadcast

Here's a story from NPR (National Public Radio). In this case, there's a brief written story at the website as well as a recording of the radio broadcast. (To document the text story, use the guideline for an internet article earlier in this chapter.) The reporter who "reads" the story on the air is listed as the narrator.

"Title of Episode." Narrator. *Title of Show*. Network, Station Call Letters. Date show aired. Medium.

WORKS CITED: OTHER

"Corning's Journey From Cookware To Gorilla Glass." Narr. Emma

Jacobs. *Morning Edition*. National Public Radio, WSKG.14 Mar.

2011. Radio.

• Abbreviate months as shown on page 165.

Kindle, Nook, and other e-readers

The MLA hasn't yet provided clear guidance for how to document e-readers, but most scholars are taking a commonsense approach. For an article, you might want to use the Internet to confirm the information you use for the works-cited entry. For a book, do the entry as you normally would (again, perhaps confirming publication information on the Internet), and then add *Kindle edition* (not italicized) to the end of your entry.

Pollan, Michael. *The Omnivore's Dilemma: A Natural History of Four*

Meals. New York: Penguin, 2006. Kindle edition.

WORKS CITED PAGE—OVERALL APPEARANCE

This chapter ends with a sample works-cited page, one that includes many of the examples you've seen so far. Note that the entries are in alphabetical order by the last name or source.

Hanging indent

One of the unusual characteristics of the works-cited page is the "hanging indent." We do it this way because the Modern Language Association tells us to, but also because it makes sense. When you have quite a few works-cited entries, it's easier for the reader to find a particular source by browsing down the left side of the page to find the author name.

You're much better off learning how to do it as I show on the next page rather than using your tab key, which almost always results in weird formatting that's hard to fix.

WORKS CITED: OTHER

TIP: WORD PROCESSING

Formatting a Hanging Indent

If you're using an earlier version of Word, see appendix, pages 240-1.

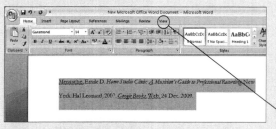

1. Start by highlighting all of your works cited entries. (It's best to do this when you're finished typing all the entries—I'm only doing one here.) Then, click on the **View** tab.

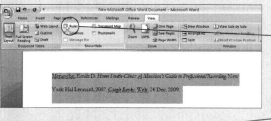

2. Check the **Ruler** box.

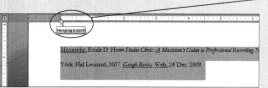

3. This little gadget is made up of three parts. You want to click on and hold the triangular one in the middle, then drag it 1/2 inch to the right.

Note: If you let your cursor hover over the boxes, it will display the function; when it says **Hanging Indent**, you've got the right one.

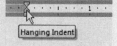

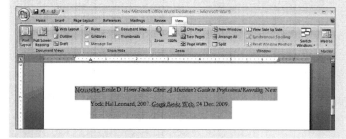

5. After dragging that triangular piece to the right, this is how it should look.

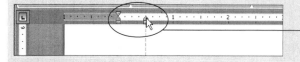

6. Done.

WORKS CITED: HANGING INDENT

Note: Double space *all* lines.

Your last name & page number

Indentation:
First line: 1 inch
Second (and additional) line(s): 1.5 inches

1 inch

1/2 inch

Cooksey 12

Works Cited

Brodhead, Richard H., ed. *New Essays on* Moby Dick. Cambride, Mass.: Cambride UP, 1986. Print.

Hughes, Langston. "Salvation." McQuade and Atwan 163-65.

McCabe, Kathy. "State Board Fines Lynn's Fire Chief over Supervision of Wife." *Boston Globe* 21 Dec. 2006: T5. Print.

Mann, Charles C. "Homeland Insecurity." *Atlantic Monthly* Sept. 2002: 81-102. *Academic OneFile*. Web. 13 June 2008.

McQuade, Donald, and Robert Atwan, eds. *The Writer's Presence: A Pool of Readings*. 5th ed. Boston: Bedford / St. Martin's, 2007. Print.

Menasche, Emile D. *Home Studio Clinic: A Musician's Guide to Professional Recording*. New York: Hal Leonard, 2007. *Google Books*. Web. 24 Dec. 2009.

Modern Language Association. "What is MLA Style?" *MLA.org*. Modern Language Association, 13 Jan. 2009. Web. 24 Dec. 2009.

Pollan, Michael. *In Defense of Food: An Eater's Manifesto*. New York: Penguin, 2008. Print.

---. *The Omnivore's Dilemma: A Natural History of Four Meals*. New York: Penguin, 2006. Print.

Shirk, Zoe. "Re: Further Thoughts on Writing Process." Message to Fred Cooksey. 25 June 2008. E-mail.

Steinberg, Shirley R., and Joe L. Kincheloe. "Privileged and Getting Away with It: The Cultural Studies of White, Middle-Class Youth." *Studies in the Literary Imagination* 31.1 (1998): 103-27. *Academic OneFile*. Web. 19 Sept. 2007.

Wolfe, Tom. "Hooking Up." McQuade and Atwan 611-18.

chapter 12

WRITERS & TEACHERS

Every writer I know has trouble writing.
~ Joseph Heller

I've always been fascinated by how writers work, so I decided to interview a couple of former students and a professional writer to hear about their processes. All three are very good writers, and Steve Waksman (a professor of music and American studies at Smith College) has published a number of books on the history of rock and roll.

The main thing I'd like you to take away from reading their interviews is how hard it is to write well—even for very smart people who seem to write easily.

The last interview is again with Steve Waksman, but this time we're talking about his work as a professor, specifically focusing on how he responds to student writing.

A WRITER TALKS
ABOUT WRITING

CANDACE CLEMENT

Writer, Activist, Musician

Photo by Seth Jackson

Candace was my student at HCC for two years, and she was also the editor of the campus newspaper (I was the faculty adviser). We eventually became friends, and now, almost five years after she left HCC, I still see her often. She was always a very good writer, but she struggled with it more when she transferred to Smith College to major in American studies. She graduated cum laude three years ago, and this interview was done during her final year at Smith.

Candace now works full-time for Free Press, a non-profit organization devoted to media reform. She also sings and plays guitar in my favorite local band, Bunny's a Swine.

Do you struggle with writing?

I don't remember struggling with writing before. Now I struggle with it more. Sometimes I struggle to come up with a thesis. My method of late has been to write lots of things—each idea is in a paragraph or two. Print it all out, cut it up.

Physically, cut it up? On paper?

Yeah. Then start rearranging it. Which is something new that I didn't do before. I think I started doing it when I had to write 25-30 page papers, which is a terrifying amount of information. I had no idea how to package it. I also do mapping. It's more picture-oriented than text-oriented. I might work on a big white board, with ideas inside bubbles, and then I draw lines or arrows from one thing to another. It's not an outline.

For example, the Russia-Georgia conflict. I had a really difficult time wrapping my head around it. I was reading about countries I'd never heard of, ambassadors I'd never heard of, leaders I'd never heard of, and I just started making columns about it, filling in names, and then making a map—this is where Russia is, this is where Georgia is, this is where South Ossetia is.

An actual map?

Not a real map, just a circle [to represent the country] dividing it up. And then, once I could see it, it made sense. I think I've shifted to being a much more visual thinker.

What do you do when you get a writing assignment? Let's say you've got a paper due on… November 1st. How do you prepare?

[Laughs.] I'd say that on October 27th, I start thinking about it.

You laugh because you know that is a *dumb* way to do it, right?

I work better under pressure. I know it doesn't work for everyone—and it doesn't always work for me. Like my thesis proposal, that's backfiring. I waited till the last minute to propose it before that first deadline, and they [thesis committee] were like, "This is an erratic mess. You need to narrow it down." I try to start with a general sense of the topic, but I probably don't come up with a thesis until I've written most of it. I might even be able to write the introduction—how I'm going to introduce the topic—and then I'll keep writing and something will kind of… emerge.

So it's not until you do some actual writing that you really know what you think.

Yeah. It's hard, because there's a tension between. . . . If you know what your thesis is, walking into it, this can be part of the problem. For example, I wrote this paper about this guy who wrote a book—I think we talked about this, his name's Andrew Keen.

Right, I remember.

So he wrote this book saying that the Internet was destroying our culture. I obviously knew what my position was, and I knew exactly how to back it up, and then I went out and found ways to back it up. So that's kind of a dangerous approach. It's not very academic.

What does that mean—it's not very academic? You're right, of course, but what does that mean?

It sounds so stupid, but it means that you need the "other sides," plural, of the story. Which, you know, I went out and found, and they just further reinforced how right I was to begin with.

A lot of college writing is "positioned" like that. That topic you described might be a special case, because it's not a traditionally academic subject. But what I think you also realize is that, academic writing means that you try to enter into things in an effort to discover.

Right. Rather than to reinforce. More of the papers I've written, it's like I said: I don't know what the thesis is going to be so I have to read about it [the subject] before I can figure that out. And then I have to start writing before I know what I think about it. I feel like I make a jump from reading to writing, and that's when I'm really thinking. I'm thinking as I'm writing. 'Cause I write, like, crazy shit. I swear, I write half sentences. I'll write furiously for ten minutes about something, and then it'll just stop. I'll run out of steam. And maybe four or five sentences out of that actually end up in the paper, but I'm like, oh, okay, that's what I think of this.

So why do you do that?

One, because some of the best sentences in the whole paper come out of that rough writing. That's the thinking process for me.

That's how it should work—writing as a form of thinking.

Right, and I'm not a very good talker.

Let me shift gears here. How does a first draft take shape for you.

I'm really bad at writing first drafts. The first draft is very stream-of-consciousness. I don't hesitate, I don't block anything.

You're not writing for an audience then. It's just for yourself.

Exactly. And sometimes, if I'm struggling with that, I'll try to write it to someone I know, like a friend of mine. "So, Tessa." She's my best friend. "This is what I'm thinking about this." And it'll help me because sometimes it gets too abstract in that stream-of-consciousness state. Then I'll go back to it a couple of days later and just—actually, wait. No, no, no. I figured it out. The first draft really is that stream-of-consciousness craziness, swearing, throwing in whatever, not finishing sentences. The second draft I'll try to take that and write it to someone else, like Tessa.

Do you ever actually send it to her? In email or something?

No, I've never done that. It's not always her, but I try to make it more verbal. So I'm not worrying about word choice and verb placement. I'll write the word *like*, I'll write the word *whatever*. I'll write *and stuff*. Because it just helps move the stream of thought or whatever along.

Explain who Tessa is, for the sake of my readers.

My best friend of ten-plus years.

What else?

Oh, she's also a student. She's very, very academic. We share that in common. She's a writer.

She's really smart, right? From everything you told me—she was living in England, taking classes at Oxford, right?

Yes.

Other people could be a really good friends, but you wouldn't necessarily think of writing to them.

True.

You'd write to her because—

It's really more that she's in the academic setting.

There you go. That's what I was going for.

She's in that world. So I know what she's looking for in an argument. ...

Right, because if you're just writing to a casual friend who's not into academic writing, maybe you dumb it down a little.

Yeah, it's really like that draft is more for figuring something out. Because you are often making an argument in a paper, and that's me figuring out how to structure the argument logically, because I know she's going to be like, *Well, wait a minute, when you say, 'the whole world,' what the hell are you talking about?* And I hear her kind of doing that in my head.

You hear her arguing with you, right?

Yeah.

And that helps you develop your thinking? Is that fair to say?

Yeah, but I don't know that it always necessarily happens in that strict an order. As in, I don't know that I always write that first draft that's crazy stream-of-consciousness and that second draft that's like, [mocking herself] "I'm writing to my friend."

It sounds like it's a messy process for you.

It's *extremely* messy, which is why I didn't really want to talk about it. It's not consistent either. It changes, and....

But that's what students need to know—that there are any number of ways of approaching writing, and finding a way that works for you is what you have to

do. So what happens after that? When does it start to turn into something that you'll hand in to your professor.

Yeah, that's usually the stuff that happens when it's really down to the wire, which I often regret. Another thing I often regret [when I'm doing research] is not flagging text when I read it. Post-it notes, sticky notes sticking out of the pages, so that I know how to find stuff later. Because I'll be thinking, *Okay, this is a great paragraph, but it really needs a sentence that backs up what I'm saying, something that's from some kind of "approved" source—a peer-reviewed journal or a book from the class or whatever.* And I often know what that sentence was, and I remember reading it, but I can't find it later, which is why it's really, really important to mark your text as you go. Not just underlining, but using those sticky notes on the pages, so you know which pages you've marked that you want to use later. I want to evolve to the point where, while I'm reading, I go, *I know I'm gonna want to use that later*, and I start writing it down, so that I have it outside of the book. But I haven't gotten there yet.

For the first few years of college, I would never do drafts of any sort. I wouldn't think I was doing drafts. But I was. I would write something, hit save, walk away and come back later. Now, there's more of a draft that happens, because I'll print something when I hit a dead end and I'll cut it up and I'll start rearranging it. Maybe I'll even split paragraphs. I'm big on short paragraphs when I'm in that process. If there's a cohesive thought that needs its own separate thing, it's in its own paragraph. And then I'll later join them and fuse them as necessary.

Or develop an idea that's maybe a very short paragraph?

Sure, or ditch it if it doesn't fit anywhere. And then I'll play with the order of it. Then I write the transitions in and out of each paragraph. Unless there are two paragraphs that really need to go in a linear fashion, I'll save the first and last sentence of each paragraph to write much later in the process.

Sounds smart.

I think that's one of the things that when people say, *This is good writing*, they mean that it transitions well. I'm not totally great at it. In fact, sometimes because I wait so long in the process, that suffers. Another thing—and this is kind of a side-note, but something I would really advocate for. It's the downside of waiting till the last minute. You *need* to walk away for several hours, if not 24 hours at a time. Not look at it, not think about it, and then read it again. And I'm really bad about doing that. The one thing you'll catch is stupid grammatical errors. That's also why it's good to have another person read it, too. Which I'm also very bad at doing. I'm insecure about my argument. I'm not really insecure about my style. But my argument—by the time it's that developed, I'm more protective of it, and I don't want to share that with anyone but the professor. But I miss so many stupid mistakes as a result of that. You know, a week after I hand in a paper, I almost always go look at it again, and say, *I can't believe I handed this in, and I can't believe I got whatever grade I got.* Except for one professor [a notoriously tough grader at Smith], who wrote on one of my papers, "I look forward to you knowing more about history." Well [with hurt look on face], I look forward to that too, I guess.

A WRITER TALKS
ABOUT WRITING

STEVE WAKSMAN

Professor, Scholar, Musician

Who knew that you could get paid to teach the history of rock and roll? Steve Waksman didn't, not when he was a student. But his interest in various forms of rock music (punk, metal, and hardcore are his areas of expertise) led him to a PhD in music, and he now teaches music and American studies at Smith College in Northampton, Massachusetts. His first book, *Instruments of Desire*, is a history of the electric guitar since the 1930s.

Let's talk about your writing. Your first book is a history of the electric guitar, which was actually your Ph.D. dissertation—the "big paper" that made you Dr. Waksman. How did that book develop? Did you know what you wanted to write when you started the research process?

The idea for the book wasn't fully formed, and it also was totally derivative [not original]—I mean, I read another book, and it inspired to me do more work on similar subject matter. Then I had to figure how to not just reiterate what someone else already said. Like, okay, someone else wrote a really good book on Hendrix. If I

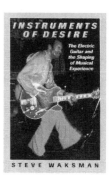

want to write on Hendrix, what am I going to say? So, I had an idea, but I didn't know how I was going to do that idea.

How do you do that? You say to yourself, "I can't just repeat what this other writer said; I have to do something original." This, for me, is the challenge for even a first-year college student.
Yeah.

You want to say something that hasn't been said. How do you do that? Do you sit around and [scratching chin in classic "thinking" pose] go, "Hmmmm…. Let me think something original."
Yeah. [Laughing.] I mean, when you're writing something like a book, you have the luxury of a certain amount of time, which allows you to think a lot, first of all. That time allows you to do that much more reading and research, and it's really in the process of doing the research that you figure out how what you have to say is maybe something that somebody else hasn't already said.

What form does that process take? Are you taking notes, writing in the margins of books?
You really want to know the process?

Yes, because I think students have this idea that professional writers sit there and think something through, and then they write it down and they're done.
Yeah.

We know it doesn't work like that, but students don't. The irony is that the professional writers I know work so much harder at writing than people who aren't good writers.
Okay, my process, in a thumbnail. This is how I do it. I read, simultaneously, as much as I humanly can. Historical background, biographies, other published scholarly work. I also do some kind of primary research—articles or other materials that are of the time period. Maybe some archival materials. And listening to music. That's phase one: Read, read, read, read; listen, listen, listen, listen. Read, read, read, read; listen, listen, listen, listen.

Taking notes?
I will start to take notes at some point. I don't ever take notes on something the first time I read it. What I do is I underline, a lot. I underline key passages. You want me to explain my underlining system?

Sure.

I underline, really, to help me go back to the book later and be able to skim it. When there's a passage that has a little more consequence to it, I put a little checkmark by it. When there's a passage that really seems like something I might want to quote, I put an X by it. And if it's a passage that I think is one of the most well-stated things I've read that I'm sure I can use somewhere, I put an asterisk by it.

So when I go back to that text, which I always do, and I take notes on it, it's that system that kind of lets me skim and prioritize what I'm skimming. I don't do note cards. All the notes I take are on full sheets of paper. Basically, in a few pages, I try to take enough notes to summarize the whole piece of what I've read. Now that's for a whole book. I do the same for an article, which of course is going to be more condensed, shorter.

Are you raising questions there? Saying, in effect, "Boy, this author blows it right here," or "She's got this all wrong"?
No—this part of the note-taking is all just summary.

For example, with the book on the electric guitar, each chapter was basically on one person, so I would research that person as much as I had time to, as much as I had the resources. I'd have, say, a hundred articles on Les Paul. I would then go back through those hundred articles, take notes on each one in a numbered list that was basically chronological, with basic information about each article—author, title, publication, date—and then a synopsis of the article, with the same kind of marking system I was talking about a minute ago. And that would basically be what I worked with when I sat down to write.

Sounds like a lot of notes, a lot of preparation before you actually started writing.
For the book I just finished, on heavy metal and punk, I have, I think, eight bound notebooks that are each about 100 pages long. So I took probably 800 pages of notes to prepare for that book.

And it's all handwritten. I don't put any of it into a computer, because the handwriting process allows it to sit in my head. I retain the information a hundred times better if I sit and hand-write and read as opposed to if I sit with my computer and type it in and look at the screen.

You're very organized about this.
Yes, and I will not start writing until I pretty much finish going through the note-taking on every source I think I'm going to need.

That sounds like an echo of the process you described using as a college student—as being "comprehensive." Get all of the knowledge so that you know and understand nearly everything there is to know about this subject that you're going to need in order to then say something. At some point in there, you must have been forming ideas of your own—"I'm going to approach it this way." Right?

Yeah. The last stage before I actually start to write is freewriting. And what happens there is that I will start to reread all my notes, somewhat selectively but also, you know, I really just try to read what I've gone through and written down. Refamiliarize myself with the material. And it's at that point that I really start to ask questions of the material and start to try to formulate ideas and arguments that I'm actually going to put into words for myself. And that I still do on paper, with a pen. I'll do as much of that as I feel like I need to. If I'm sitting down to write a chapter of a book—and I very much write chapter by chapter—I will start to freewrite, and I'll basically try to frewrite to the point where I feel like I have the makings of a thesis. And that may take me a page, a couple of pages.

I don't outline the whole chapter. I used to. When I was in college and I first started writing long papers, I would outline the whole thing from beginning to end. I wouldn't necessarily stick to it, but at least I had the structure. I don't do that anymore. Now I just need the starting point. What's my thesis? What am I trying to say in this chapter?

And I also, in that free-writing process, try to figure out what I'm going to start with. If I'm going to write a fifty-page chapter on Les Paul or Jimi Hendrix or Motorhead, or whomever it is, what's the thing that's going to get me into that chapter? What's going to get my reader interested but will also introduce my themes, so that I can work my way into stating my thesis and my argument without wasting too much time.

You know, you could be talking about a five-paragraph paper as easily as a book. Which is one the lessons I hope students will take away from hearing you talk about your process. What writers of book-length works are doing isn't altogether different from what writers are doing in a much shorter form. What you talk about at the chapter level is also true at the paragraph level for an essay.

That kind of gets to another part of my process. My actual writing process is similarly meticulous to my note-taking process. I basically write paragraph by paragraph. I don't sit down and write ten pages and then reorganize. I sit down at the computer and try to write the best paragraph that I can. It usually takes me an hour, or maybe two, to write a really good paragraph. In any given day, I will rarely do more than two paragraphs. I write roughly a page a day, every day, for as long as I'm working on a particular project.

A chapter, it'll take me two months usually, writing a page a day, if it's a page a day. I take no breaks, no weekends.

Meaning, you work on weekends.
Yes. And I also work on school things, on teaching. If I'm teaching, I try to sit down in the morning, or maybe at lunch, whenever, find time—even if I write a half paragraph. It's better for me to do some writing on any given day than not to, if I'm in the process. Because it just helps me keep that continuity. I prefer to do it in the morning, when my brain is fresh. The rest of the day, whatever else I'm doing, somewhere in the back of my mind I'm thinking about that piece of writing… and thinking about what should come next.

So I don't outline, but I write paragraph by paragraph, and after each paragraph I spend basically twenty-four hours thinking about what the next paragraph should say.

It doesn't really mean that I'm right, or that I make the best decisions, but that meticulousness has worked well for me over time. I don't go on twelve-hour writing binges, I don't "half-write" in a way so that it eats up whole weeks at a time. It just kind of folds into my ordinary day. Which is also something that is useful for a student to think about. You don't just have to cram it in. If you have a certain kind of discipline and work style that will allow it, you can kind of allow the writing to just be a part of what you do—as opposed to this thing you have to make this absolutely crazy-ass effort for. You know, it took me a while to develop that way of writing….

What you say about time, I think, is really important. Students do themselves a disservice, and make the process much less rewarding than it could be, when they try to cram all this work into a day… or less. Writing should be kind of interesting, kind of compelling, and it's hard for it to feel like that if you're under this awful deadline. It takes any pleasure that might exist—and I know that's a foreign concept to most students, the idea of pleasure and writing—and kills it. Is there pleasure in it for you?
Definitely. Although it's certainly a labored kind of pleasure. A lot of deferred gratification. Most of the writing process feels like you're getting to a place that you're never going to get to. *If I could just get to this place….* In my head I know it's there, but it just keeps eluding me. And, most days when I write I don't really get there. I may write a nice paragraph, and I'm happy about that, but I know I haven't really said the thing I've set out to say.

You don't even know what that thing is necessarily, right?
Right. Really, there's only a few times in a chapter where you really say the thing that above all is what you want to say. Most of it is getting there. At least in my writing. You can't just keep saying your main point over and over again—you're getting there. And that can be both pleasurable and frustrating, because you want to just get there, you want it to be over with. Come on! But for me, I can't hurry it. I can't just jump five steps ahead and be like, "All right, I just said it." Because if I don't put the work into getting there, it's not going to feel like I said it the way I wanted to say it.

How does revision factor into your process?
On the book I just finished, I did a substantial revision after I did a full draft. The first draft that I wrote was good, but it was a little all over the place. I hadn't fully focused my ideas and my arguments.

Who can, in a draft?
Yeah, well, it was a big first draft. It was 400-and-some-odd pages. I would have liked there to be some focus. There was some focus, but definitely when I revised it I had the feeling of, "Ah, that's what I really wanted to say."

What's going on when you revise? You know, you've got this whole thing, you look back over it, whether it's eight pages or 400. You look back over it and you know it's deficient in some way; it's not quite doing what you want it to do. What happens next?
Well, first of all, some of that comes from other people's opinions. My editor was reading it while I was working on it, giving me feedback. She'd say, "This really works well," or, "This doesn't work so well." And she wouldn't say, "Change it like this." She'd just say, "Work on it." So it was up to me to figure out what that meant. What I did in that book, that I didn't do in the first book, was I got very into telling stories that ultimately weren't necessary to the point I was trying to make.

Maybe they were necessary. Maybe they helped you learn something about your subject.
Yeah, I think they were. They fit into some vision I had of the project that was probably what motivated me to do it, but when it came down to trying to focus more, some of that stuff seemed a little less important when I went back and looked at it. You know, "That's a neat story, but it goes on for four pages, and it doesn't go anywhere that great."

Did you cut most of them?
I cut a good bit of it, yeah.

Was that difficult?
Yes, it was.

You've heard that expression about "killing your darlings"? [A reference to the need to get rid of writing that you're proud of but that doesn't serve enough of a purpose.]
[Laughing.] It is a little like that—"Why do I have to get rid of it? What are you talking about?" Yeah, and I can get defensive about that too. But… I allowed my ego to do what it needed to do, and then I looked at the stuff with a fresh eye, and what happened was that I started to recognize that I needed to take some stuff out. But it wasn't just a matter of deleting stuff. It was a matter of restating stuff, or perhaps reorganizing stuff, so that it wasn't exactly the same story. And when I did that, it was like, "Oh, yeah, this is more along the lines of what I wanted to say." So deleting stuff was one part of it, but it was really more about how big pieces of it fit together in a way that was more economical, more focused, but still had a lot there. The book is still 400 pages. I cut probably 10 percent. There was a lot to be able to cut, and still feel like there was a lot there.

As a teacher, you know the problem for students—for them, often, revision means correcting the spelling errors and putting commas in the right places. But that's not what you're doing when you revise.
Right, not at all. I need time to be able to go back to something I wrote and read it in a way so that everything that's there doesn't just make automatic sense to me.

You have to see it fresh.
Yeah, and it takes a while for me to see that. Because when I've spent two months writing something, my first impulse is to say, "I'm done, and it's really good, and I'm happy with it, and I just want to put it away."

I bet we could come up with a formula. Maybe you need to leave at least equal time before you try to revise. So if it took you a month to write it, you better give it a month before you try to read it and think about it critically.
Maybe. But some of that would depend on whether or not you were getting other feedback. I didn't really do significant revision until I got some feedback.

A WRITER TALKS
ABOUT WRITING

NICHOLE REYNOLDS

Graduate Student

Nichole Reynolds left college when her son, Nate, was born fifteen years ago. Six years later, she had a daughter, Sadie, who's now nine. For much of this time, Nichole worked as a waitress, but she held onto the idea of returning to college. At thirty-three, Nichole began taking courses at Holyoke Community College, in Holyoke, Massachusetts. Two years later, she received a full scholarship to attend Mount Holyoke College, one of the most respected colleges in the country. She maintained a 3.98 GPA (that's all A's and a single A-, by the way) at Mt. Holyoke and graduated in spring 2011. She will enter the PhD program in English at UMass in the fall of 2011.

What follows is the transcript of my (2008) interview with Nichole about her writing process. I chose Nichole because she produced some of the best student writing I've ever read. She's lucky in that she loves language, but she's also an extremely hard worker.

You're a very good writer now. But I seem to remember you telling me that you used to struggle with it.
When I went to UMass-Amherst [in the early 1990s], I was a horrible writer.

Really? By your standards or . . .
My problem was that I didn't know my audience. I was trying to impress rather than write from my heart.

How did that change?
Partly life experience. Part of it is just reading what's expected of me a little bit better. Just reading the assignment.

Really? The assignment?
Exactly.

Tell me about your process.
I freewrite. That's key. I take a day and say, "I'm not going to try to put anything together. I'm just going to write."

Some students say they don't want to freewrite because they just end up with— I'm quoting them here—a bunch of crap. How do you get around that?
A lot of it *is* a bunch of crap, actually. Then I pull the things that I think are borderline not crap, and I work with them. Probably only ten percent of my freewrite makes it into my paper. From that ten percent, I can get a sense of what style or voice I might use for the paper, and who my audience is. That guides the next step that I take. I do a lot of cutting and pasting. I usually have four or five documents open, and I just keep pulling and pasting until I start to see an outline. Writing is a really visual thing for me. I wake up at night and I can see the loose ends sticking out. I actually have a tape recorder next to my bed so I can get my idea down on tape. [Laughing at herself.] I know that's way more than what most people would do, but that's what writing is for me. It's a feeling, and I can feel when something's not right. I need to give myself a lot of time when I write. That part takes three or four days.

You do one thing, I think, that most college writers don't do—you start days or weeks before a due date. How important is that?
Incredibly important.

So many students make themselves miserable, I think, because they put papers off so long. But writing can be enjoyable—when you have time to really dig into your subject. It can be rewarding—but I'm going to stop talking because you have something to say.
I do! I don't like writing, actually. I like having written. That's from Dorothy Parker [a twentieth-century American writer]. I don't like writing. I struggle because . . . I think that part of it is because I'm a perfectionist. The other part of it is that when you're writing really honestly—and that's the only way to write—is to really connect to what you're writing. Then it's something inside of you on a page for people to read, and that's tough to do. It's tough to expose yourself that way.

Maybe you've been lucky, at least recently, that you've been able to write about things that you cared about.
I think so. But last semester I had to write a paper for a combined history-psychology class. So I had to write about history, which I don't like, and psychology, which I don't know about. That was hard for me to do. I didn't really feel connected to the topic, so it was hard.

How'd you get around that?
I fell back on what you warned me against doing, which was not being clear or direct enough, because I didn't feel like I had a clear line to my topic. So I wrote around it, and they called me on it.

You knew you were doing that.
I did. And I didn't feel good about handing the paper in. Even though I gave myself plenty of time to work on it, it just wasn't what I . . . . You have to be connected to your topic. You have to feel something about what you're writing about, and I chose wrong.

If you had it to do over again, what would you do differently?
I would choose a topic that I felt like I could express myself through.

Sometimes I think students could look harder to find a way into a topic.
I agree.

They say, "Well, here's my assigned topic, and I have no interest in that at all." But wait—maybe you tweak it a little bit and find something you are interested in.
Absolutely.

What about later stages of the writing process?
That's the worst part. When I'm doing bigger papers, you know, more than seven or eight pages, I have a hard time considering it as a whole. I try to do a lot of editing within paragraphs but then it makes it dissonant with the whole thing.

So you're struggling to get that big picture view.
Yeah, that's the most important part of writing for me, to make it a cohesive whole.

So how do you do it, or attempt to do it?
I go through a lot of black ink cartridges, printing and looking, pulling out pages and reworking something and adding something. And I read my paper dozens of times before I'm done. I think it out. I need thirty minutes, and I'll do something different, and then usually it comes to me—"Oh, yeah, that's what I wanted to do." But if I sat in front of that screen any longer, I wouldn't have found it. You know, I needed to walk away. Writing needs to be a long process. Whether it's five pages or fifteen, it's a couple of week kind of thing, I think. I don't know how people do it when they say, "Oh, I did this last night."

What about reading? How does that influence your writing?

I spent years before going back to school reading—the *Utne Reader* [a magazine that collects and publishes articles from a variety of publications], The *New Yorker*, cover to cover. I found myself mimicing some of the writers. I circle words that they use that I like and think about how I might be able to work with them.

Any final thoughts? Advice for students who are struggling?

If I were talking to students about writing, I'd say, "Give yourself time. Don't wait." It's going to be twice as good if you just give yourself enough time. Cause you know what's not right. You read it and you say, "Hmmm." Even two days later—I usually finish my paper a couple of days ahead of time, and I go back and I read it and I say, "Oh, well, I knew what I was saying then, when I was *in* the writing, but as a reader, I can't see that connection." So I fix it.

Thanks for your input, Nichole, and good luck at Mt. Holyoke.
Thanks....

A PROFESSOR TALKS ABOUT
GRADING STUDENT WRITING

STEVE WAKSMAN

Associate Professor of Music and American Studies
Smith College

What do you find that students don't understand about writing, particularly early in their college careers?

There are a few things. One, they don't always understand that they need to make an argument, and if they understand that they need to, they don't always understand *how* to. So, for instance, the difference between an opinion and an argument is not always clear to some students. You know, that making an argument doesn't just mean, "I think this." It means working something out. That's one thing.

Perhaps a bigger issue that I see in a lot of my students' writing—and this is something I put a lot of emphasis on—is how to use evidence. It seems like when I read, especially first-year student papers, with few exceptions, which are the ones who really seem to know what to do, I get one of two extremes, which is either the paper with no quoted evidence, or the paper with nothing but quoted evidence. [Laughing.] So, my comments are either, "You need more evidence," or, "Stop quoting so much and use your own voice a little more." And I think they're two different things. The student thinks, *Well, I read this stuff and I kind of know what it says, so if I just kind of summarize it, it's fine.* You need to show that you've read it, but also you need to show that you've read it carefully, thoughtfully, gone to it, and found real direct evidence as opposed to a synopsis of something. Those students, I think, are sometimes a little overconfident. The other ones are underconfident: "I don't really know what I'm talking about, but we read a bunch of stuff and if I quote enough of it, my professor will think that I know what I'm saying." But it's like, *You didn't actually say anything yourself.*

And the student maybe thinks, "Well, at least the professor will know that I read everything I was supposed to read."

Yeah, exactly, which is important. But it's only one part of what you're there for. So I think that's something students need a lot of work to figure out—what's the best balance between putting forth something in your own words but also marshalling the evidence you have. And it's not just evidence, right? It's also the text as something that can stimulate you to say something that much more clearly and authoritatively than you may otherwise say it, if you find the right quote. So I work with my students—cultivating their sense that they should be using the words of others, but that they should be doing so not just in this flatly, evidentiary way. Not, *Here, look, I read it,* but students need to do something with it.

It's what we were talking about earlier. The writer has to be present; you have to know why this paper is being written. I find the same kind of problem—it's in the lack of *interaction* with the source material.
One of the things that happens most often, and it's not a *grave* error, but to my mind, it's usually an error, which is you use a quote to make your point, and then you don't say anything more. So I think, one of the hints is, Don't assume the quote, even if it says what you want to say, says all there is to say. You are using that quote in the service of something *you're* trying to say, so you should make it clear how that quote fits in with what *you* want to say. Not just let it speak for you. So paragraphs, to my mind, especially in a college-level writing situation, should almost never end in a quote. Put the quote in there, but then have something that you've extrapolated from it, because then you're making your own meaning out of it.

What's going on intellectually or psychologically when you grade a student's paper?
[Long pause.] Ummm....

I think the intellectual part might be pretty easy, but the psychological part, I think students don't know what's going on in our heads when we grade papers.
Well, I guess part of that is I'm priming myself for a certain amount of repetition—because if I'm grading, whether it be eight papers in a class, or twenty or forty, among those papers a lot of it is going to be more or less the same. So, psychologically, a lot of it is reading a paper, trying to set aside the stuff that's just like every other paper, and look for the stuff that is more . . . . What is *this* student saying? What is there about this paper that isn't just fulfilling the assignment in the most basic way but is actually bringing something a little bit more to it. A lot of papers don't bring that much more. [Laughter.]

So then it's a matter of, *Well, what are you giving the student credit for?* How much credit should they get for just having done the assignment, in a sort of reasonably good manner? And how much are you really expecting that they should have gone a little beyond? I try to strike the best balance between those I can, because sheer completion counts for something, and it takes effort. But when you read a paper that has clearly—either because the student is just a little more advanced or the student worked that much harder, or some combination thereof—when you read a paper that really does go a little beyond what you might have even expected, or at least beyond the basics of what you're asking for, it really stands out. So, psychologically, you just feel . . . good: *Wow, that student really got it.*

And you feel good as a teacher because you want to take at least a little bit of credit for it. But you also feel good that you passed on a certain amount of knowledge that somebody has then taken and made something of on their own. And that is relatively rare. In a group of, say, twenty papers for me, maybe four of them will do that. So, most papers are fairly routine, and that's okay, but students who write routine papers—if they're surprised when they get a grade back, they should maybe try to figure out what the expectations are, or.... I mean, it's tricky. You don't want to go to the student who got the good grade and be like, "What did you do?" But you've got to somehow, if you care, as a student, If I didn't do that, how do I do it? And I don't quite have many students willing to at least come to me to do that, even at a school like Smith where we supposedly have pretty motivated students—a very small proportion actually will come to me and say, "You told me I did this wrong and I kind of understand why, but could you help me figure out how to do it better."

Watch video interviews of professors talking about grading:

facebook.com/quickanddirty

chapter 13

READING AND WRITING
ABOUT LITERATURE

The answers you get from literature
depend on the questions you pose.
 ~ Margaret Atwood

So, you don't love literature? I didn't either.

When I was in 10th grade, I had a very demanding English teacher who made us read a number of nineteenth century British and French novels. It was one of those "gifted and talented" classes, and because I had always been good at English, it was natural that I would take it. I hated it. I remember forcing myself to sit in a chair in my parents' living room and read George Eliot's novel *Adam Bede*. Well, kind of reading it. Mostly just letting my eyes move rapidly over the words and waiting for it to be over. I got nothing out of that novel, just like I got nothing out of *Les Miserables* (though I found it slightly more engaging, at least), *Great Expectations*, and many other "great" novels.

I asked to be moved into a "regular" English class, and after some resistance from my teacher (who thought I was lazy and needed a challenge), my request was granted.

This experience did not exactly give me a deep love of literature, and it makes me sympathetic to those of you who come to literary study with indifference, repulsion, fear, etc.

My love of literature did take hold, but only I after I read novels and plays that spoke to me more directly. I also had some great teachers (thank you, Robert Bausch). My point is that if you've never liked reading novels, stories, poems, or plays, you should try to keep an open mind.

Where do they come up with this stuff?

You're in class, discussing a poem, and someone says, "Clearly the car symbolizes his desire to escape the trappings of modern American life." Or something like that. Something that makes sense once it's been explained but that you never would have thought of on your own.

That can be intimidating. And it can also feel like a game, one in which some people have the secret decoder ring (the one that unlocks all of the "meaning" of a particular work) and you don't. It can make literature unpleasant, something to be avoided. Who wouldn't want to avoid it if it just makes you feel stupid?

I have two pieces of advice for you. First, don't worry about the fact that some people seem to have an easier time making sense of literature. Second, remember that sometimes your classmates are, well, full of it. (Sometimes your professors are, too, but that's another matter.)

The question is, how do you develop the skill of literary interpretation? Because it *is* a skill. That's the purpose of this chapter, and I could have also named it *learning to see what's not there,* because I'm trying to get you to think about the most basic ways of reading: literally and figuratively. To read literally is to understand the plot and the basics of character. You understand "what happens" in a story, poem, or play, but you don't necessarily understand what any of it *means* in a deeper sense. And that's the key, because literary works (unlike more popular books) are ultimately concerned with *meaning.* For the most part, literature does not explain its meaning. It gives you enough clues—in details of character, action, imagery, and so on—to let you figure it out for yourself, to come to your own conclusions. So first, make sure you understand the surface of the work before you try to delve deeper. Understanding the "surface" is what the next part of the chapter is concerned with; following this, I'll walk you through an analysis of a story and a poem to illustrate how to take the next step toward understanding meaning.

THREE STRATEGIES TO GET YOU STARTED

1. Cheat a little.
2. Figure out where you are.
3. Identify "characters."

1. Cheat a little.

First, let me be clear about what I *don't* want you to do: I don't want you to go to Google and find a summary, analysis, or interpretation of any work you've been asked to read. Yes, those are easy to find, but if you read them before attempting to make sense of a story or poem yourself, you won't get much out of this. And if you "borrow" from one of those ready-made essays, that is the kind of cheating that can get you in real trouble. (See discussion of plagiarism on pages 109–10.)

When I suggest that you "cheat a little," what I mean is that you should do a little background research on the author and the time/place in which the story was written or set. Many textbooks have a brief biography of authors before their works. If not, do a quick Google search. If the poet is German and the poem was written in 1920, there's no chance she's writing about, say, nuclear war. Of course, knowing that a poem was written in Berlin in 1920 doesn't tell you a whole lot, but it should help you narrow down the likely possible "worlds" of the poem.

In the case of a story like John Updike's "A & P," it's essential that you think about what life in (predominantly white, upper-middle class) America was like in 1961. If this is a period you don't know much about, do a little research. In that story, for example, the history of the bikini in America is highly relevant; here's one piece of research I found on the topic: "The 1960 popular song, 'Itsy Bitsy Teenie Weenie Yellow Polka Dot Bikini' was a direct reflection of how widespread this swimsuit style was becoming in the popular American marketplace."

2. Figure out where you are.

In other words, roughly, what's the setting? You should be able to orient yourself to the "world" of the story, poem, or play—are you in a city, in the country, the suburbs? On an airplane, in a hotel room, inside a tent in the middle of the Sahara? Stories and poems both rely on images, and most writers work hard to create precise ones. Try to picture these images as fully as you can, as if they're a movie playing inside your mind.

The other aspect of determining where you are might be called plot, though I'm reluctant to apply this word to poetry because poems don't usually have a plot in the way that stories typically do. But do think of the "events" of the poem; what's happening here, what are the actions and interactions? It's often helpful to state the plot as plainly as you can, just to make sure you understand it at the simplest level.

If you understand how stories are shaped, it might help you make sense of them more easily. Most stories follow a structure that is either character-based or action-based; some combine both structures.

Character-based structure

1. Character wants something.
2. Character is opposed (by another character, by some outside force, or by something within himself or herself)
3. Character overcomes some or all opposition.
4. Opposition increases or changes.
5. Crisis point: Push and pull of forces come to a point where they can't keep going back and forth.
6. Resolution: Character gets what he or she wants, or doesn't; sometimes, resolution is less clear.

Plot-based structure

1. Everything is fine.
2. Something goes wrong.
3. Situation is corrected—to some degree.
4. New problem occurs, or original problem returns in new form.
5. Crisis point: Push and pull of forces come to a point where they can't keep going back and forth.
6. Resolution: Things are made right, or not; sometimes, resolution is less clear.

Note: In both cases, steps 2-4 can be repeated many times.

See my "jagged line of narrative" on page 210 for more on how plot works in fiction.

3. Identify and analyze characters.

This terminology belongs to fiction, but poems do often have *characters*, at least in a sense. As you're reading, identify the people in the story or poem and their likely relationships. With stories, remember that the author is never one of the characters in the story. (Okay, there are a few exceptions to this, but those are in the realm of "meta-fiction" and you most likely will not encounter them in an introductory literature class.) In a story, there's generally a *protagonist* (the main character) and one or more *antagonists* (someone who opposes the protagonist). Authors rarely come right out and tell you what to think of a character; instead, you have to figure out what kind of person you're dealing with based not only on what they say, but also how they dress, what they eat, and so on. The details are important. If a father is described by his young son as having a "thin, pale throwing arm," you should be able to guess that the boy perceives his father as somewhat weak.

The jagged line of narrative—and "The Three Little Pigs" as example

The "jagged line of narrative" is my way of describing how almost all stories rely on increasing tensions, leading up to the crisis point.

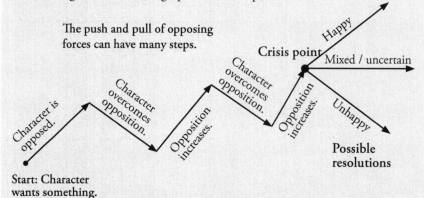

1. *Characters want something:* The three pigs are sent out by their mother to live in the world on their own; their most basic desire is for survival.

2. *Opposition:* Mother tells them to be careful and protect themselves from the wolf. Note: The opposition hasn't yet appeared in the story; it exists merely as a threat at this stage.

3. *Characters overcome opposition:* To protect themselves against the threat, they build houses: one of straw, one of sticks, and one of brick.

4. *Opposion increases:* The wolf blows down the first two houses and eats the first two pigs.

5. *Character overcomes opposition:* The wolf is unable to blow down the brick house—sadly, only the third pig overcomes the opposition.

6. *Opposition increases:* The wolf comes down the chimney.

7. *Crisis point:* The push and pull of forces has gone as far as it can (at least in this story), and something must happen to resolve the increasing tension.

8. *Resolution:* The pig starts a fire in the fireplace and boils a big vat of water, which the wolf falls into, killing himself. A happy ending for the third pig.

Just for fun: Search the Internet for *wolf's side of the story*—there are some interesting versions of "The Three Little Pigs" told from the wolf's perspective. Think about how this reinterpretation of the story changes both the tensions and the meaning.

Poems have "characters" too, though generally not in quite the same way that stories do. Begin by thinking about who is "telling" the poem. If the poem is written in first person (using "I"), we call this person *the speaker*. The speaker is frequently—though not always—the author. Does the speaker interact with other people? If so, who are they and how are they connected to the speaker? Are they family members, friends, coworkers, strangers?

FICTION

The key thing to remember about fiction (and drama) is that it's all about conflict. Without conflict (or tension, or a problem), there's no story. This is how story-telling has always worked because we're naturally interested in how people respond to problems, and how problems get resolved. It's how we learn about life.

Literary works are always trying to "teach" us something. This doesn't mean that they have some simplistic "moral" like "Do unto others as you would have them do unto you." In serious literature, the "lesson" is never so simple. Many teachers say that literature is interested in exploring "the human condition." That's true, but I also believe that serious literature often has a simpler goal: to show us that our understanding of some aspect of life is incomplete. Often, in the most respected works of fiction, we are left slightly confused about what it all means. You should get used to this feeling.

SAMPLE STORY ANALYSIS: "BUTTERFLIES"

Find the short story "Butterflies," by Patricia Grace online. (A Google search for *Patricia Grace Butterflies* should work.) It's a very short story, just a page long. I'll use the three strategies from the previous pages to begin the analysis, then examine conflicts more closely.

1. Cheat a little.

The first time I read this story, I assumed it was set somewhere between the 1940s and 1960s in the American South; I also assumed, with relative certainty, that the granddaughter and her grandparents were African American, while the teacher was white. Imagine my surprise when I learned that the author was from halfway around the world, New Zealand, and that she was of Maori descent. This changed some of my ideas about the story, but it also allowed me to think about the universality of the story's themes. (By *universality* I mean the ways in which various interpretations of the story can be applied not just to one time, place, or group of people.)

In order to understand the people in this story, I did some research on the Maori people and learned that they are an indigenous people, and that they have experienced conflicts with Europeans (particularly the British) quite similar to those experienced by African Americans in the U.S. The Maori lived primarily in rural areas until at least the 1960s, and this seems to fit with Grace's story, which was written in 1985 (and which perhaps recalls an earlier time or depicts a family still living in a rural area). I also did some research on butterflies and agriculture and learned that in New Zealand (and maybe elsewhere; I'm not much of a gardener so I didn't explore further) white cabbage butterflies cause significant damage to cabbage plants.

2. Figure out where you are.

Even though I was originally mistaken about the country in which the story likely is set, I knew that the setting was the country, and the time was likely some decades ago. So, the plot: A young girl who lives with her grandparents goes to school for the first time. At school, she writes a story (and/or draws a picture) about killing butterflies. When she gets home, she tells her grandparents about it. They expect that the teacher would have liked the story, but the teacher didn't. The grandfather says that this is because the teacher buys her cabbages at the supermarket.

That's a summary of the plot. Have I revealed anything more meaningful about the story? No, so I need to go further. But I probably can't do much more with just the plot—I'll need to look more closely at the characters.

3. Identify and analyze characters.

Who are the people (or animals, in some cases) and what kind of lives do they lead? How are they connected to each other? In conflict with each other? What do they want?

Girl: She's very young, and she seems eager to please both her grandparents and her teacher. She doesn't know that a story about killing butterflies will upset her teacher. Why doesn't she know this? Because she comes from a rural tradition where butterflies are a nuisance.

Teacher: We don't know much about her, but we can assume that she's not familiar with the traditions of the girl's family and their way of life.

Grandparents: They are simple people; most likely they do not have much formal education (they speak ungrammatically), but they have great respect for it (they tell the girl, firmly, to obey the teacher). At the end, though, the grandfather suggests that the teacher does not understand something about their way of life, namely that she doesn't realize the threat that butterflies pose to cabbages.

4. Examine conflicts between or within characters

Girl vs. Teacher: Yes, but it's the simplest and most obvious conflict here.

Grandparents vs. Teacher: Yes, in a sense—see "abstract conflicts" below.

Girl vs. Grandparents: Not exactly, or at least not yet. Maybe later in life the girl will be in conflict with her grandparents. (The grandparents might glimpse this possibility at the end of the story.)

Grandparents vs. Grandparents: In other words, they are in conflict with themselves, also known as an internal conflict. (I don't mean that the grandparents are in conflict with each other; rather, the grandfather is in conflict with himself, and the grandmother is in conflict with herself.) This is the most important conflict in the story, and the one that makes it a good example of literary fiction because in literary fiction the most significant conflicts tend to be *within* characters. These happen when a character is being pulled in two or more directions and the choices are not easy.

Here's the nature of their internal conflict: The grandparents want the girl to do well in school (and in life), so they put their faith in the teacher. But when they learn that the teacher doesn't know about how butterflies can endanger their food supply, they question whether or not they should have this faith in her. (No, this is never discussed in the story, so you have to imagine the inner life of the character.)

5. Examine abstract conflicts

In order to get to the deeper meanings in literature, you often need to look for abstract conflicts, those between opposing ideas, ideologies, belief systems, and so on.

In this story, the most important conflicts are those that are represented by the grandparents and the teacher. Start by thinking about all the ways in which they are different from each other.

Life Experience vs. Formal Education: This is a classic conflict, one that is present throughout American life and literature: the clash between "street smarts" and "book smarts." As I'll discuss below, this conflict also leads to one of the great ironies of this story, namely that in spite of her supposedly superior formal education, the teacher actually lacks knowledge possessed by the grandparents.

Tradition vs. Progress: The grandparents have, in effect, embraced "progress" by sending their granddaughter to school rather than keeping her on the farm. But by the end of the poem, they are perhaps wondering how much faith they should put in "progress" if it means losing the knowledge of how to grow food. More specifically, this can be seen as a conflict between rural/agricultural ways of life and urban/technological ways of life.

Minority / Marginalized Peoples vs. Dominant Culture: For me, this is the most significant and important conflict in the story, particularly the way in which the teacher, as representative of the dominant culture, confidently "corrects" the girl's "error." The teacher not only fails to understand the intelligence of the marginalized culture, but she makes no attempt to understand that culture.

Final analysis

This story fascinates me on a number of levels. And there's a great irony in it, as well: the grandparents would seem uneducated to many readers, but it's actually the teacher who is lacking in awareness. Also interesting is that the teacher is obstinate in her ignorance—she doesn't attempt to understand the "intelligence" of the girl's culture but instead simply dismisses it as wrong. This irony becomes apparent to the grandfather by the end of the story, when he seems to be rethinking the high regard in which he has held formal education. Beyond this, though, I think the grandparents are forced to reevaluate their entire view of the dominant (meaning: in terms of political and financial power) culture in that time and place. The story could also be read as a moment of awakening for the grandparents (and, more universally, for any "marginalized" culture), one in which they may begin to assert the value and wisdom of their own cultural traditions.

Try to make the story relevant to your life: Many students have been pushed to do well in school and go to college by parents who did not attend college themselves; the parents don't necessarily know what is being taught in that "world," but they put their faith in higher education because they believe that it's the key to a successful life. So what happens when the students begin to learn about politics, culture, war, and so on, from a perspective that doesn't fit with the parents' world view (or for that matter, with the worldview of students' friends who didn't go to college)? What happens, for example, after a student reads "The Excrement Poem" on the first day of my class, and then goes home to tell her Catholic friends or parents how the poet has declared that the natural world is not governed by God but by cycles of life? Now, do you see how the themes in "Butterflies" are more universal—and potentially relevant to you or people around you?

POETRY

Poems can be difficult, often because language is used in unfamiliar and sometimes perplexing ways. My most basic advice is to take your time—poems require rereading, often many times. In addition to the three strategies I discussed earlier in the chapter, I'll add two more here, specific to poetry.

1. Cheat a little.
2. Figure out where you are.
3. Identify "characters."
4. Pay attention to line breaks.
5. Pay attention to metaphorical language.

4. Pay attention to line breaks.

A poem is broken into stanzas, and each stanza is made up of lines. Notice how most poems can be read as a collection of complete sentences—but poets don't always "break" the lines in predictable places, and when they don't, you can guess that the poet wants to call attention to something. This technique is called *enjambment* or a *run-on line*. For example, in a poem about her relationship with her teenage daughter, Sharon Olds writes:

> **My daughter—as if I**
> **owned her—that girl with the**

These first line is *enjambed*, meaning that it ends in an unnatural place. The second line does the same thing, but that enjambment is less signficant. A natural place to end a line is after a mark of punctuation (period, comma, etc.), but these lines from Olds stop in places that are jarring to the rhythm of the poem.

Because of this, they call attention to the words that end the first line ("as if I") and the words that begin the next line ("owned her"). Olds could have written

> My daughter—as if I owned her,
> that girl with the

In short, by breaking the first line where she does, Olds is emphasizing the words "as if I"; so you should ask yourself why. In this case, the answer, at least in part, is that the enjambment causes the reader to detect a kind of equation: daughter = I. Olds is saying that when she thinks of her daughter, it's as if the daughter is Olds herself. Plenty of parents do this, right? They think of their kids as extensions of themselves, and this is exactly how Olds is thinking in that first line. But if she hadn't enjambed it, this meaning would not be present. The enjambment also places extra emphasis on the next words, "owned her," calling attention to the idea of possession. In fact, the title of the poem is "The Possessive."

5. Pay attention to metaphorical language.

Language is at the heart of poetry—you have to examine it closely. Pay particular attention to nouns and verbs, and focus on short phrases and even single words.

Later in that poem by Olds, she describes her daughter's new haircut as being like a "helmet." Ask yourself why Olds would choose this particular object to compare her daughter's hair to. What's a helmet for, and who wears one? Mainly a helmet is for protection, of course, but from what? In this case, other language in the poem helps establish a pattern: it's as if the daughter is a soldier going into battle (against the mother). This metaphor reveals something very specific about how the mother is perceiving her daughter: as an adversary, someone with whom she is about to be at war.

SAMPLE POEM ANALYSIS—"DIGGING"

Find the poem "Digging," by Seamus Heaney, online. (Search for *Heaney Digging poetry foundation*. This site has the text of the poem; many online sites don't have the poem itself.)

1. Cheat a little.

You should be able to learn that Heaney was born in 1939, that he grew up in a rural area of Northern Ireland, and that his father was a farmer and cattle-dealer. Heaney published "Digging" in 1966, when he was just 27 years old. From this, you might guess that the poem will not be about a mid-life crisis or old age (at least not his own).

2. Figure out where you are.

In the first stanza of "Digging," the speaker (not narrator) is holding a pen, and he's looking out a window. He says he looks "down," so he's probably on the second floor. I assume he's sitting at a desk. Then he tells you what his father looks like as he works in the flowerbeds.

"Where you are" isn't just about place—it's also about time. Notice that Heaney says that his father's rump comes up "twenty years away." In other words, now he's thinking back to twenty years ago. The verb tense also changes here from present to past tense.

Then, the speaker recalls his father in the past before moving to recollections of his grandfather.

The last two stanzas are back in present tense, presumably the speaker again at his desk, thinking about digging in a new way.

If you read the biographical note, you also know that Heaney is Irish; it therefore seems fair to assume that this poem is set in Ireland, and that some of the memories are of a time when his family worked the land for their living.

3. Identify "characters."

There's the speaker, his father, and his grandfather. The grandfather is compared to other men in the area, but they're not discussed directly. Sometimes it's helpful to think about who's not present in a work—in this case, wives, mothers, girlfriends, sisters, etc. In other words, no women. Remembering the era in which the poem was written, the exclusion of women might make sense because the poem is fundamentally concerned with how one's "work" is connected with one's sense of identity and purpose.

4. Pay attention to line breaks.

The last line of the second stanza is

> My father, digging. I look down

You should be asking yourself why Heaney would break that line (after the word *down*) in such an awkward place. This enjambment is made even more powerful because it occurs between stanzas—there's a huge rhythmic pause between the end of this line and its continuation in the next stanza ("Till his straining rump among the flowerbeds"). What does this mean for you as the reader? It means that Heaney wants you to notice that the speaker is looking down on his father, most likely in a purely physical sense (the speaker is on the second floor) but, more importantly, also in the sense of feeling superior. Without enjambment, that extra sense would not be present, or at least not nearly so noticeable.

5. Pay attention to metaphorical language.

Why, in the second line, does the speaker describe his pen as "snug as a gun"? Why would he compare the pen to a gun? And why would it be snug? When you think of something that fits the hand snugly, what do you think of? A pair of gloves, most likely. Probably not a gun. So you have to ask yourself why Heaney wants you thinking about a gun at this moment.

Play word association: For a moment, forget the poem and just think about the word "gun": write down as many words as you can think of that you associate with "gun." Examples: violence, death, crime, hunting, power, etc. Once you've done this, then go back to the poem and ask why the poet would want you thinking about these things in connection with the speaker's pen.

The answer is that in this moment, the pen carries the metaphorical power to *kill* the traditional ways of working with the earth—digging, planting potatoes, harvesting peat, and so on. As the speaker sits at his desk, thinking of himself as a writer, thinking of himself as superior to his father, he perceives his pen as a weapon against the physicality of farm labor. It's also possible to view the pen as a defensive weapon; in this view, the speaker doesn't necessarily want to kill the tradition, but merely to defend himself against the expectation that he will work the land in the same way as his ancestors.

WRITING ABOUT LITERATURE—THREE GUIDELINES

Entire textbooks are devoted to writing about literature, but my goal here is simply to help you get started.

Avoid plot summary

When you write about literature, your audience is other people who have read the work you're analyzing. Therefore, you don't need to tell them what happened in the story, poem, or play.

In some cases, you may need to mention an element of plot in order to make a point about it; if so, that's fine, but be sure to keep the plot summary to a minimum—your comment *about* what happens should be the focus.

Analyze

This is the key to writing about literature. In short, to *analyze* means to look closely at the parts of something. In "Butterflies," for example, you might analyze the language patterns of the grandparents. You should have noticed, for example, that they speak ungrammatically, specifically in their misuse of standard verb forms such as "Do as she say." If you start to analyze all of their speech patterns, you might also observe that they don't always break grammatical rules but that they do tend to speak simplistically.

Before you begin to judge them, though, you should think about how these character traits indicate something other than stupidity. They may be "simple" people (at least from our perspective), but they also know things that the teacher doesn't. This analysis of language can lead to an exploration of larger tensions in the story.

One of the simplest ways to do analysis is to find particular parts of the story that you can't explain. Assume that everything is there for a reason and that every element contributes to the work as a whole. Focus on small elements—phrases, single words, images. In general, say more about less.

Develop a primary insight into the work

Thinking about how the characters are presented in the previous analysis of "Butterflies" should naturally lead you to larger questions and insights into the work. In an informal piece of writing, such as a response your professor wants you to write before discussing the work in class, you might begin by saying something like this:

> Patricia Grace's "Butterflies" is about the tension between two ways of life.

In a more fully developed paper, a more specific thesis statement would be appropriate:

> Patricia Grace's "Butterflies" uses a simple, child-like situation to explore the tensions experienced by marginalized people as they struggle to face the difficult question of assimilation—both its rewards and its costs.

The key feature of these two sentences is that they are both interpretive assertions about the story. Both are judgments that will need to be supported with the writing that follows.

While some writing teachers suggest writing your thesis statement first, I think this is often difficult. It makes more sense to me to write at least some of the body of the paper (even an informal paper) and then let that help determine what your "primary insight" will be.

Writing about literature is not so different from other kinds of writing you've been asked to do in freshman composition—in both, you want to make an assertion (the thesis) and then support that assertion with appropriate evidence, examples, and so on.

One of the biggest problems I find with student writing is a lack of depth. Many papers tend to say a little about a number of different topics rather than exploring more deeply into a limited number of ideas. Don't settle for just saying that the grandparents speak ungrammatically. Look more closely at all of their speech and think about what else you could say. Look for patterns (they use a lot of simple, direct commands with the girl) and disruptions to patterns (the last sentence, which is far more complex than anything else the grandfather says). Challenge your initial impressions (e.g., *the grandparents aren't very smart*). In short, don't just skim the surface analytically—dig in and force yourself to explore beyond your first ideas.

READING LITERARY CRITICISM

If you need to use secondary sources for a paper, your professor should give you guidelines. I'll simply offer a few suggestions about how to approach reading literary cricism—and how to use it in your paper.

Once you've found an appropriate source, you should read with two goals in mind: first, to deepen your undestanding of the literary work being examined, and second, to determine where the critic is offering opinions, interpretations, and judgments about the work.

Critical essays always provide some background on particular work(s) or author(s), and they also often summarize the positions of other scholars. But one of the main things you should look for is an argument by the scholar you're reading. All literary criticism seeks to present a view of the work (or the author, or the time period, or the genre—or some combination of all these) that the critic wants you to accept. Just as when you read other types of writing (newspaper articles, editorials, etc.), be sure to differentiate between fact and opinion.

In the example from Arthur McGuinness's essay on Seamus Heaney below, can you tell what is fact and what is opinion?

WHY DO THEY CALL IT LITERARY CRITICISM?

Most writing about literature falls under the heading *literary criticism*, and the term can be misleading because the word "criticism" suggests being critical of something. But in this case it means to look closely, to examine. (Book reviews are slightly different because they do tend to "pass judgment," but literary criticism doesn't typically do this.) The goal of literary criticism is to see literary works in new ways— to make historical, artistic, political, and cultural connections; in short, to understand them more fully.

> The poems in [*Death of a Naturalist* and *Door into the Dark*] are generally more direct, less figurative, less allusive, and less literary than those in *Wintering Out* and *North*. In his first two volumes he proposes to dig into the darkness of the earth and his own imagination with his spade-pen to discover his roots. Knowing that Heaney was born a Roman Catholic and attended Catholic schools until he went to the university, one might expect the traditions and rituals of that faith to have a central place in his poetry. But actually there is little reference to Catholicism.

The first sentence is a judgment about Heaney's early work, therefore an opinion. The second sentence, too, is opinion—it offers an interpretation, a way of seeing those first two books. In other words, not everyone would agree with McGuinness's characterization of the books.

The information about Heaney's Catholic faith is largely that: information. The last sentence is more debatable—it seems like the kind of assertion that could be proven simply by looking for references to Catholicism in the poems; if you find few, then the statement seems factual. Still, it wouldn't surprise me if some other critic found a way to disagree with this "information"; he might argue that in fact there are plenty of references to Catholicism but that they are less obvious, more symbolic.

In other words, the line between information and argument is often blurry.

INTEGRATING SOURCE MATERIAL INTO YOUR ESSAY

Generally, there are three approaches to integrating literary criticism into your writing. One is to find something that supports a view you hold; another approach is to find something with which you disagree; and the third approach is to extend a critic's idea.

Using supporting material

In a 1980 essay, critic Jay Parini writes that Heaney's first collection shared Philip Hobsbaum's "bias toward lean, physical language wedded to intellectual toughness." I don't know who Philip Hopsbaum is, but I like Parini's description of Heaney's language, and I think it's similar to something I might say about Heaney's writing. So here's how I might integrate Parini's assertion into my essay:

> Heaney's imagery and language often contain a kind of masculinity, a strength, that can be seen in such phrasings as, "By God, the old man could handle a spade." Jay Parini has made a similar observation, calling Heaney's language "lean, physical."

Notice that I begin by offering my own analysis, and that what I have to say is at least slightly different from what Parini says. My assertion doesn't simply rephrase Parini's—in its focus on masculinity, it says something new.

Note: I didn't have a parenthetical citation because I named Parini in the sentence, using a signal phrase ("Jay Parini has made a similar observation"); also, because I read Parini's essay in a database (rather than in the actual, printed journal), I did not have access to a page number and therefore did not include that information at the end of the sentence.

Using material you can argue against

Another approach to criticism is to find an assertion with which you disagree. Parini goes on to call *Death of a Naturalist* "an apprentice volume," which I find belittles the work unfairly. Here's the quotation:

> *Death of a Naturalist* is an apprentice volume, one in which a young poet tests the limits of his abilities, tries out various verse forms and metrical patterns.

I might address this in an introduction or conclusion, someplace where I'm making more general assertions about the work, but you can certainly find more specific assertions to argue against within the body of your paper as well. My interaction with the quote might read like this:

> While Parini views the first collection as "an apprentice volume," this view fails to take into consideration the self-awareness with which Heaney constructs many of these poems; Heaney may occasionally appear youthful and immature, but these moments are a ruse behind which hides a more careful and mature purpose.

Again, there's no parenthetical citation; see explanation in previous note.

Extending a critic's idea

Often, you'll read something by a critic and agree with it up to a point but then find that you think about the issue slightly differently. Scholars do exactly this all the time, responding to other scholars by saying, in effect, "Well, he's right about this, but he doesn't quite go far enough." The key is to find an assertion that you mostly agree with but which you can also question. I'll illustrate with a quotation from critic Michael R. Molino in reference to "Digging":

> The fact that the father has some kind of "rhythm" implies the naturalness of his actions, although it could be the speaker's perception of the father being in harmony with nature, a trait the speaker feels he does not share.

I agree with Molino's interpretation here, but I don't feel that he's taken the idea far enough. To make a new point, I examine other language and imagery from those same lines, and I come to a slightly different conclusion:

> Michael R. Molino accurately characterizes both the father's "harmony with nature" and the speaker's lack of connection to this father's work. But in neglecting the speaker's undignified description of the father's physical motions—his "straining rump" as it "bends low," and his "stooping"—Molino underestimates the speaker's distaste for his father's labors.

The key to what I've done in my extension of Molino is to agree with some of his ideas, but then to offer a different analysis, one that goes beyond—and in fact disagrees with—Molino's views.

Final thought

One pattern you should have noticed in my use of source material is that in each case I found a way to *interact* with the quoted material. This is the key to writing a paper that is analytical rather than just a summary. In order to make sure that you're doing this in your writing, keep asking yourself, *What do I have to say about that?* You can't rely only on well-chosen and insightful quotations—you also have to offer your own insight.

FINDING LITERARY CRITICISM

USING GOOGLE SCHOLAR

Google has become increasingly useful for legitimate research, as you'll see over the next few pages. But it's also potentially dangerous. A simple Google search for *heaney digging* returns a few links to the poem itself and a number of student essays on the poem, many of them for sale for ten or fifteen dollars. Yes, you can easily download a ready-made essay on this poem, but keep in mind that if it's easy for you to find an essay like this, it's also easy for your professor to find it too. (See my comments on plagiarism on pages 109–10).

In short, a basic Google search for literary criticism is generally a bad idea. Instead, start with Google Scholar. Use the pull-down menu on the Google page called **more** to get to it.

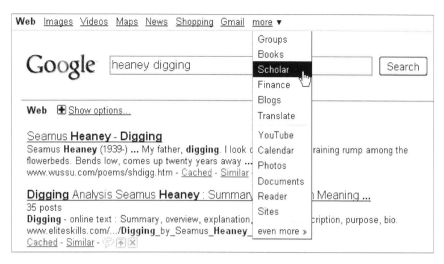

What you should be looking for is literary criticism by a scholar, someone who is an expert on Heaney's work. Browse the titles and descriptions, looking for language that connects with the themes in the work you're writing about. If you were writing about "Digging," for example, some of the prominent themes would be land, ancestry, tradition, poetic identity, voice, and so on.

Many of the results below would not be appropriate as literary criticism specific to Heaney's early poetry. The first one, however, is good—I like the fact that it's from a publication called *Critical Quarterly*.

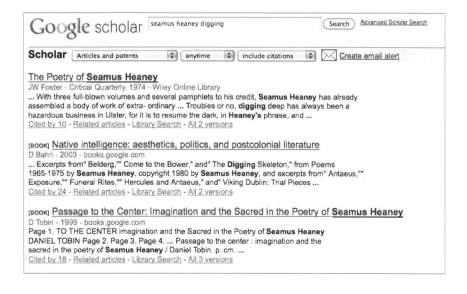

This is just one page of results—there were many, many pages. Typically, I found one or two essays on each page that might be useful.

Be aware that you may need to use broader search terms. "Digging" happens to be a very well known poem, one that many critics have written about. If you don't find anything after putting in the name of the poet and the title of the story or poem, try searching for the title of the collection of stories or poems, or by author name and keywords (for these, think thematically, as I did on the previous page).

Note: Often you'll come across links, like the one below, to subscription services—which means you'd have to pay to get access. They'll show you the first page of the article, but not all of it. If this is the case, make note of the author, title, and other publication information so that you can look it up in one of the library databases (which I explain in a few pages). Or try the *All __ versions* link, explained below.

> JSTOR is a subscription service, and typically you would have to pay to read this article. Many colleges do subscribe, though, so check with your professor or a librarian to see if your college has access.

The Gift and the Craft: An Approach to the Poetry of **Seamus Heaney**

E Andrews - Twentieth century literature, 1985 - JSTOR
... 131). Early poems like "**Digging**" and "Follower" establish his troubling self-consciousness about the relationship between "roots and reading," the lived and the learned. ... 374 Page 8. THE POETRY OF **SEAMUS HEANEY** confidence ...
Cited by 3 - Related articles - All 5 versions

> Increasingly, Google is providing other ways of finding the article. Where it says *All 5 versions*, click on this link to see if some other site has made the article available. I tried the fourth one, and it worked.

The Gift and the Craft: An Approach to the Poetry of Seamus Heaney
E Andrews - Twentieth century literature, 1985 - JSTOR
In a 1981 interview with John Haffenden, Heaney remarked: "It's possible to exacerbate.... I believe that what poetry does to me is comforting. ... I think that art does appease, assuage." In Field Work the poet, newly "landed in the hedge-school of Glanmore," renews his commitment ...
Cited by 3 - Related articles

The Gift and the Craft: An Approach to the Poetry of Seamus Heaney
E ANDREWS - Twentieth century literature, 1985 - cat.inist.fr

The Gift and the Craft: An Approach to the Poetry of Seamus Heaney
E ANDREWS - JSTOR
In a 1981 interview with John Haffenden, Heaney remarked: "It's possible to exacerbate.... I believe that what poetry does to me is comforting. ... I think that art does appease, assuage." In Field Work the poet, newly "landed in the hedge-school of Glanmore," renews his commitment ...

[PDF] The Gift and the Craft: An Approach to the Poetry of Seamus Heaney
E Andrews - Twentieth Century Literature, 1985 - saintbonaventure.com
THE POETRY OF SEAMUS HEANEY it to his attention: he immediately relates it to the sound of water gushing from the pump in the yard of the farm where he was brought up. The source of his imaginative power, we are to understand, lies in his rural childhood experience that ...

[PDF] The Gift and the Craft: An Approach to the Poetry of Seamus Heaney
E Andrews - Twentieth Century Literature, 1985 - saintbonaventure.com
THE POETRY OF SEAMUS HEANEY it to his attention: he immediately relates it to the sound of water gushing from the pump in the yard of the farm where he was brought up. The source of his imaginative power, we are to understand, lies in his rural childhood experience that ...

USING GOOGLE BOOKS

Another option is Google Books. Use the pull-down menu called **more** to get to it.

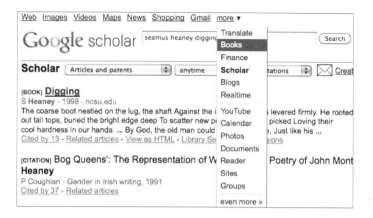

The results of the Google Books search included quite a few textbooks, which are not what you should be looking for here. Two results, though, appear to be scholarly, and both examine "Digging" specifically.

Seamus Heaney - Page 29
Harold Bloom - 2003 - 111 pages - Google eBook - Preview
Here he remarks on Heaney's imagery that presents the similarities of working with pen, plough, spade and many other instruments of labor.] Since his first acclaimed poem, "**Digging**," **Seamus Heaney** has considered writing as work. ...
books.google.com - Add to My Library ▼

Seamus Heaney: the crisis of identity
Floyd Collins - 2003 - 246 pages - Google eBook - Preview
In this study, Floyd Collins develops a model of crisis that proves an apt tool for assessing Seamus Heaney's poetic career.
books.google.com - More editions - Add to My Library ▼

Either of these would be good to investigate further, but I'll start with the second book because it has the word "identity" in its title (and because this was one of the words that I suggested earlier might be a thematic keyword for a search).

After clicking on the link for the book, make note of the search field on the left side of the screen. Here, you can enter the name of a specific poem, or one of the thematic keywords. To keep it simple, I've entered *digging*.

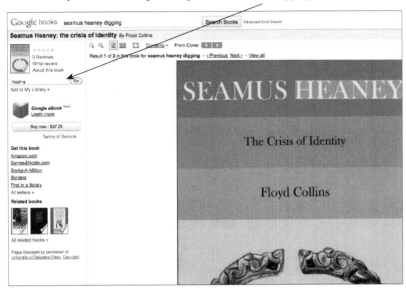

After clicking Go, Google Books will display a partial page image of each place where the word *digging* appears in the book. The first two references look relevant and useful, while the third does not. **Note:** Google Books won't let you look at every page of most books. Find the book in the library (see Chapter 9) if you can't see what you need in Google Books.

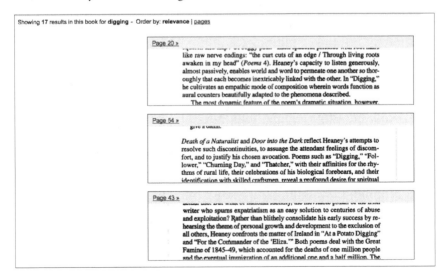

USING DATABASES

See directions in Chapter 10 for how to get to the databases.

Many databases are devoted to literature, but I'll show you how to use the one that I believe is easiest and most comprehensive, the *Literature Resource Center*.

Other good databases are *Bloom's Literary Reference Online, Literary Reference Center,* and *Contemporary Literary Criticism.*

HOW *NOT* TO SEARCH IN A DATABASE

Note: Do not try to use search terms in the same way you do with Google. Generally, you should use only one term (or maybe two if you do an advanced search).

The first page you see is called a **Basic Search**. This is good place to start.

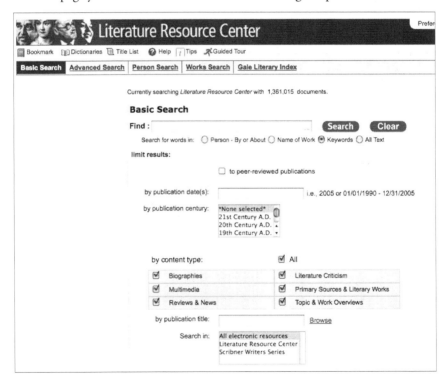

Enter the writer's name in the search field, and select the option that says
Person—By or About.

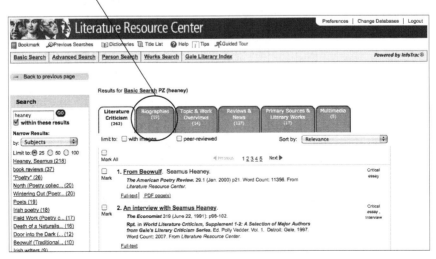

You could just start scrolling through the results, but there are quite a few of
them, so this probably isn't the most efficient way to proceed.

Look at the tabs and see how the results are divided. The default is **Literature
Criticism** (262 results)—but I think you should have some background before
you get into the criticism.

Select **Biographies**.

The *Dictionary of Literary Biography* (fifth, below) is often a good place to begin your research.

The article by Robert Buttel from the *Dictionary of Literary Biography* is an overview of Heaney's entire life and career, and it's quite long. It's all worth reading as background, but if you want to locate the parts of the article that will be most relevant to your research, see my tip on the next page.

YOUR NEW BEST FRIEND = CTRL F

In long articles, you can quickly locate references to a specific word by using the computer's **Find** function (CTRL F). You should read the whole article, of course, but this will help you find where the author specifically refers to the word *digging*, which is highlighted (in color) wherever it appears. Simply hit the Return key to see the next place where the word appears.

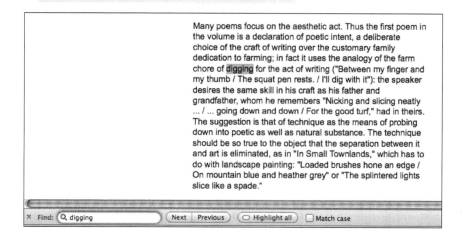

Now, return to the Basic Search results, where I'll show you how to narrow your results.

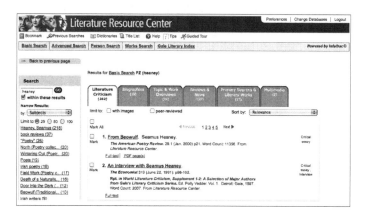

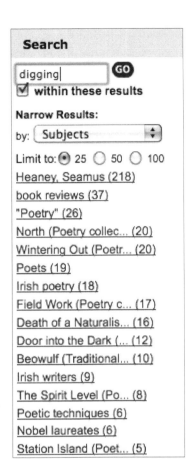

On the left, you'll see a variety of ways to narrow your search, which is a good idea here because Heaney has been writing poetry for more than forty years, and much of the criticism will not be relevant to the early work that includes "Digging."

I used the word *digging* in the search field, and you can see below that this limits the results to eighty; many of these, like the first one, are still not specifically about the poem, but quite a few are.

Note that the third and fourth results are brief "critical essays"—you'll find these for many stories and poems. They're useful, but because they're written specifically for students, they're not really literary criticism in the traditional sense.

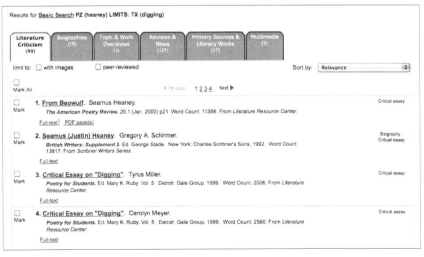

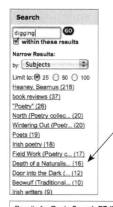

At this point, the best strategy is to find the name of the book that "Digging" was published in. A quick Internet search tells me the collection is *Death of a Naturalist*.

I click on that title here.

Now the results are reduced to sixteen, and many of them are excellent, especially the first, fifth, and sixth articles below. See next page for further analysis.

Results for **Basic Search** PZ (heaney) LIMITS: SU ("Death of a Naturalist (Poetry collection)")

Literature Criticism (16)	Biographies (19)	Topic & Work Overviews (14)	Reviews & News (127)	Primary Sources & Literary Works (17)	Multimedia (5)

limit to: ☐ with images   ☐ peer-reviewed   Sort by: Relevance ▾

☐ Mark All   ◀ Previous   1   Next ▶

☐ Mark **1. The Poetry of Seamus Heaney**. John Wilson Foster.   Critical essay
   Critical Quarterly, Spring. (1974): p35-48.
   Rpt. in *Contemporary Literary Criticism*. Ed. Carolyn Riley and Phyllis Carmel Mendelson. Vol. 5. Detroit: Gale Research, 1976. Word Count: 1983. From *Literature Resource Center*.
   Full-text

☐ Mark **2. *Wintering Out***. Elmer Andrews.   Critical essay
   The Poetry of Seamus Heaney: All the Realms of Whisper. Houndmills, England: Macmillan, 1988. p48-81.
   Rpt. in *Poetry Criticism*. Ed. Michelle Lee. Vol. 100. Detroit: Gale. Word Count: 14178. From *Literature Resource Center*.
   Full-text

☐ Mark **3. From *Winter Seeds* to *Wintering Out*: The Evolution of Heaney's Third Collection**. Michael Parker.   Critical essay
   New Hibernia Review 11.2 (Summer 2007): p130-141.
   Rpt. in *Poetry Criticism*. Ed. Michelle Lee. Vol. 100. Detroit: Gale. Word Count: 4384. From *Literature Resource Center*.
   Full-text

☐ Mark **4. Violence and Silence in Seamus Heaney's 'Mycenae Lookout.'**. Elizabeth Lunday.   Critical essay
   New Hibernia Review 12.1 (Spring 2008): p111-127.
   Rpt. in *Poetry Criticism*. Ed. Michelle Lee. Vol. 100. Detroit: Gale. Word Count: 7698. From *Literature Resource Center*.
   Full-text

☐ Mark **5. Seamus Heaney: The Ground Possessed**. Jay Parini.   Critical essay
   The Southern Review 16.1 (Jan. 1980): p100-123.
   Rpt. in *Contemporary Literary Criticism*. Ed. Jean C. Stine and Bridget Broderick. Vol. 25. Detroit: Gale Research, 1983. Word Count: 2688. From *Literature Resource Center*.
   Full-text

☐ Mark **6. 'Hoarder of Common Ground': Tradition and Ritual in Seamus Heaney's Poetry**. Arthur E. McGuinness.   Critical essay
   Éire-Ireland 13.2 (Summer 1978): p71-92.
   Rpt. in *Contemporary Literary Criticism*. Ed. Dedria Bryfonski and Laurie Lanzen

Now I have some good results. Notice the titles of these articles—they should remind you of the thematic concerns that I discussed earlier in the chapter. I'm particularly interested in #5 and #6 because they both refer to the "ground," which is closely connected, thematically and conceptually, with "Digging."

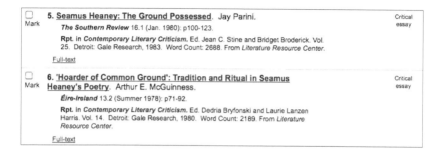

Other factors I pay attention to are the length of the article and information about the journal.

Length of article: These two articles are 2000–3000 words, which is an ideal length for literary criticism: long enough to have depth, but short enough to be manageable.

Journal information: Both of these publications are academic journals, which is the kind of source you want to use in a literary analysis paper. Even if you're not familiar with the name of the journal, you should notice the way the publication dates are written: 16.1 (Jan. 1980) for the first, and 13.2 (Summer 1978) for the second. This format virtually guarantees that these are academic journals, because they publish seasonally and number the publication by volume and issue (e.g., volume 16, issue 1).

Conclusions?

Within just 10-15 minutes of searching, I found a broad overview of Heaney's work (*Dictionary of Literary Biography*), two short essays specifically on "Digging," and at least three legitimate pieces of literary criticism, all of which are highly relevant to the subject matter in the poem.

appendix

MICROSOFT WORD PRE-2007

The word processing tips found throughout this book use more recent versions of Microsoft Word. In this appendix, you can see how to do a variety of formatting and other functions in the earlier versions of Word. Also, if you don't have Word on your computer and don't want to pay for it, I highly recommend Open Office. It's a free program that functions almost identically to Word. The Website is www.openoffice.org.

TIP: WORD PROCESSING

Saving as RTF: Rich Text Format

Computers can be unpredictable, especially when you're moving from home to school or a friend's house to work on a paper, print, etc. I highly recommend that you save your drafts in Rich Text Format, which will ensure that you can open your paper on any computer.

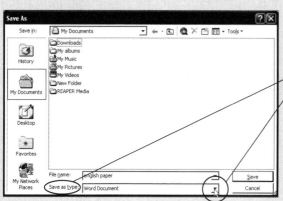

First, choose Save As under the File menu. When you see this screen (left), go the box at the bottom called *Save as type*. Use the arrow to pull down that menu, and then scroll down to *Rich Text Format.*

TIP: WORD PROCESSING

Creating a header with page number

Many students have trouble with page numbers and headers. Here's how to do it. Start by pulling down the *View* menu and selecting *Headers and Footers*.

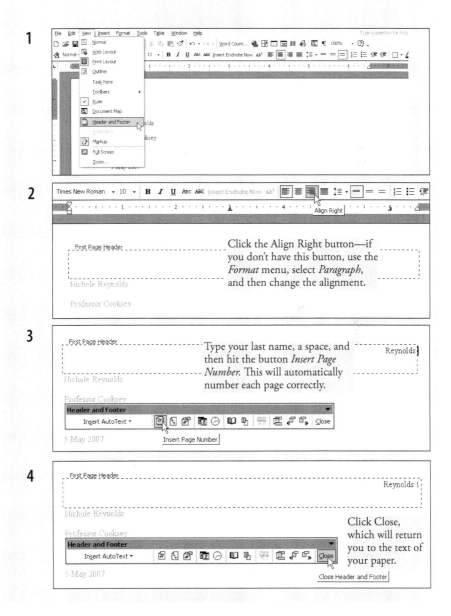

TIP: WORD PROCESSING

How to format a block quotation

If you have a ruler at the top of your page...

1 First, highlight the block quote. Then, grab the bottom of the small box on the ruler bar (let the cursor hover over it—if it says *Left Indent*, you've got the correct one) and move it half an inch to the right.

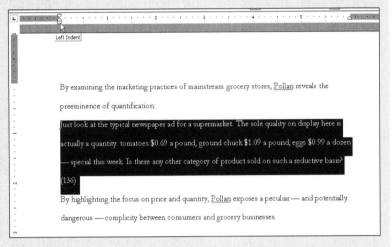

TIP: WORD PROCESSING

How to format a block quotation

If you *don't* have a ruler at the top of your page…

1 First, highlight the block quote. Then, under the *Format* menu, choose *Paragraph*.

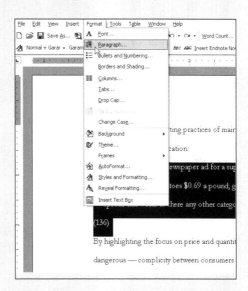

2 Under *Indentation*, increase the left indentation to 0.5". Hit OK and you're done.

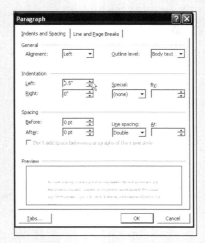

TIP: WORD PROCESSING

How to format a hanging indent

Start by highlighting all of your works-cited entries. (It makes sense to format them all at once when you've finished writing them.)

If you have a ruler at the top of your page...

1 Find the little triangle pointing up—before you click it, just let the cursor sit over it; when it says *Hanging Indent*, you know you've got it.

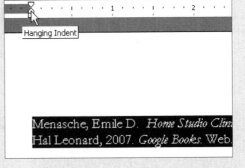

2 Click and hold that triangle, then drag it a half-inch to the right. Don't forget to double-space, too.

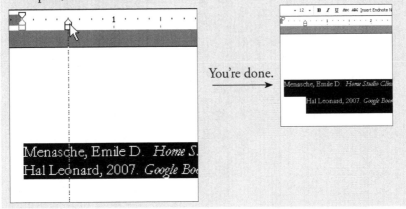

You're done.

TIP: WORD PROCESSING

How to format a hanging indent . . . if you *don't* have a ruler at the top of your page.

1 Start by highlighting your works-cited entries (see previous page). Then, go to the *Format* menu and select *Paragraph*.

2 Under Indentation, find the box that says *Special* and change it to *Hanging*.

3 In the box to the right, labeled *By*, set it to 0.5".

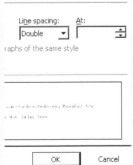

You're done.

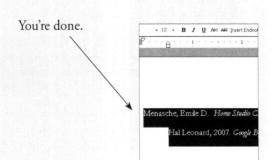

Index

Made in the USA
Charleston, SC
06 August 2011